# TRUE LOVE

*Parental Alienation Cannot Erase the Many Memorable Moments of a Mother's TRUE LOVE For Her Children*

Dr. Marni Hill Foderaro

Copyright © 2024 Dr. Marni Hill Foderaro.

All rights reserved. No part of this book may be used or reproduced by any means, graphic, electronic, or mechanical, including photocopying, recording, taping or by any information storage retrieval system without the written permission of the author except in the case of brief quotations embodied in critical articles and reviews.

Balboa Press books may be ordered through booksellers or by contacting:

Balboa Press
A Division of Hay House
1663 Liberty Drive
Bloomington, IN 47403
www.balboapress.com
844-682-1282

Because of the dynamic nature of the Internet, any web addresses or links contained in this book may have changed since publication and may no longer be valid. The views expressed in this work are solely those of the author and do not necessarily reflect the views of the publisher, and the publisher hereby disclaims any responsibility for them.

Any people depicted in stock imagery provided by Getty Images are models, and such images are being used for illustrative purposes only. Certain stock imagery © Getty Images.

ISBN: 979-8-7652-5142-3 (sc)
979-8-7652-5143-0 (hc)
979-8-7652-5141-6 (e)

Library of Congress Control Number: 2024908105

Print information available on the last page.

Balboa Press rev. date: 11/28/2024

# TRUE LOVE

**Parental Alienation Cannot Erase the Many Memorable Moments of a Mother's TRUE LOVE For Her Children**

*"The greatest legacy we can leave our children is happy memories."*

*~ Og Mandino,*

*American Author & Salesman*

# CONTENTS

DISCLAIMER ........................................................................................................... vii
DEDICATION ....................................................................................................... viii
A HEARTFELT NOTE FROM THE AUTHOR ............................................................ x
AUTHOR BIOGRAPHY .......................................................................................... xv
MOM'S MANY MEMORABLE MOMENTS ........................................................... xxi

A ............................................................................................................................ 1
B ............................................................................................................................ 5
C .......................................................................................................................... 15
D .......................................................................................................................... 25
E .......................................................................................................................... 29
F .......................................................................................................................... 33
G .......................................................................................................................... 39
H .......................................................................................................................... 45

| | |
|---|---|
| I | 51 |
| J | 55 |
| K | 59 |
| L | 63 |
| M | 69 |
| N | 77 |
| O | 81 |
| P | 85 |
| Q | 95 |
| R | 97 |
| S | 101 |
| T | 111 |
| U | 117 |
| V | 119 |
| W | 121 |
| X | 125 |
| Y | 127 |
| Z | 129 |
| PHOTOGRAPHS & MEMORIES | 133 |

*"Photographs and memories.
All the love you gave to me.
Somehow it just can't be true.
That's all I've left of you."*

**~ *Jim Croce,***

*American Singer-Songwriter*

# DISCLAIMER

*"Take care of all your memories. For you cannot relive them."*

**~ Bob Dylan,**

*American Singer-Songwriter*

This memoir book falls into the realm of creative writing, where there is a storytelling aspect to its contents. It contains emotional truths and perspectives of the author's lived experience. The photographs were taken by the author and the memories shared are from the author's viewpoint of her experiences. Memories are imperfect. Childhood memories can be contrived and rewritten by alienators. The author does not mention any names or show images of people other than herself to protect individuals' privacy and to maintain the anonymity of others. All of the characters, businesses, objects, places, events and incidents in this book are either the product of the author's experience or imagination and/or could be used in a fictitious manner. Any resemblance to actual persons, living or dead, or actual events is purely coincidental. The identifying characteristics of some people described in this book have been modified or changed. To the best of the author's ability, she has re-created events, locales, people, objects and organizations from her memories of them. The author and publisher make no representations or warranties of any kind with respect to the contents in this book and assume no responsibility for errors, inaccuracies, omissions or any other inconsistencies herein. They hereby disclaim any liability to any party for any loss, damage or disruption, whether they result from negligence, accident or any other cause. Reading this book is at your own risk and you agree to take full responsibility for any resulting consequences. It is implied in the genre of memoir that this book is written through the eyes of the narrator, and small details of fact may be incorrect or conflated. The use and reading of this book implies your acceptance of this disclaimer.

# DEDICATION

*"Sometimes memories sneak out my eyes and roll down my cheeks."*

*~ **Bhavya Gaur,***

*Author & Spiritual Intuitive*

This 8th and final book in the TDFL series

*TRUE LOVE*
*Parental Alienation Cannot Erase the*
*Many Memorable Moments of a Mother's*
*TRUE LOVE For Her Children*

is lovingly dedicated to
our son & our daughter

**from their mom who loves them BOTH so very much!**

# A HEARTFELT NOTE FROM THE AUTHOR

*"Sometimes you will never know the value of a moment until it becomes a memory."*
*~Dr. Seuss/Theodor Geisel,*
*American Children's Author & Cartoonist*

Being a mother, raising our two beautiful children, is the purest form of unconditional love and most rewarding experience I've ever had. Words aren't able to fully express the **TRUE LOVE** that I have for our son and daughter.

Even before our kids were born and decades later into their 20s and 30s, I created detailed scrapbooks filled with photos, mementos and sentiments to capture their special moments, milestones, accomplishments, interests, feelings and experiences, to preserve and cherish their memories.

**Memories play a role in our overall well-being.**
**Memories strengthen our sense of identity and purpose.**

These personalized keepsakes for our son and daughter were meant to safeguard their memories, so our children's recollections would reflect the many positive moments in their wonderful lives. I didn't foresee that there would be a future time when these memories would be all that we had left, because I never anticipated that after close to three decades of marriage I would endure the unbelievable heartache and significant losses that come with being a severely Targeted Mom, unable to protect our children from extreme Parental Alienation.

It's important for me to stay loving, remain honest and continue to act as a positive role model for our son and daughter, even from afar. Our kids are doing the best they can to survive this devastating form of Child Abuse.

My wish is that the many memorable moments and colorful photo collages I included will help our children remember the numerous magnificent experiences they had in their childhood and positive times they shared with me. I decided that this 8th volume,

*"TRUE LOVE:*
*Parental Alienation Cannot Erase the*
*Many Memorable Moments of a Mother's*
*TRUE LOVE For Her Children"*

would be the final book in the *"TRUE DECEIT FALSE LOVE"* series. I hope and pray that our kids will read this special keepsake book I lovingly created for them.

There's really no end to a mother's memories. Just when I think I've listed them all, many more pop into my head that I feel should be added which would jog our kids' recollections, encourage them to critically think, pull on their heartstrings and remind them of the love and happy times shared between us. The same is true with images of things we did, places we went and adventures we experienced. So, since this book of memories could potentially go on "to infinity and beyond," I chose to put my pen down on our daughter's 29th birthday.

I remember our daughter as intelligent, worthy, capable, lovable, funny, loving, kind, happy, hard-working, creative, morally ethical and empathetic. I pray that her heart, mind and soul will awaken to the truth, dispelling the lies she's been told by the Alienator, and the many enabling friends and family who helped solidify the Alienation. I hope she will someday realize that her mom loves her and has always loved her unconditionally.

*It's been over a decade. I miss you so very much.*
*You will always be my beautiful and sweet Kiss-Girl.*
*I love you forever and always.*

This book of memories is also for our wonderful son. I sincerely want him to feel good about himself, be emotionally and financially independent, be physically and mentally healthy, surround himself with positive people, follow his dreams, pursue his passions and make it on his own. He's intelligent, worthy, capable, lovable, funny, loving, kind, happy, hard-working, creative, morally ethical and empathetic. I believe that he does know that his mom loves him unconditionally.

***Stay strong, be honest, work hard, remain compassionate and let your own intuition guide you towards happiness, health, independence and personal growth.***

***You will always be my handsome and smart Sweety-Ding.***
***I love you to the moon and back.***

Memories and feelings of certain events are unique for each person, even though they may be experienced simultaneously with two or more people. So even though I've conveyed events and experiences that I, as a mom, deem significant and positive, that may or may not hold true and be the same for our children. To complicate matters, our kids can be influenced by others to alter the way they view situations or relationships. A well-known alienating strategy is to "rewrite our children's memories." False Memories are a common factor of Attachment-Based Parental Alienation where there are shared delusions with the Favored Parent against the Rejected Parent.

Our unique human brain encodes, saves, retrieves information and connects that information to our past experiences and present feelings or state of being, which then impacts our future responses, thoughts and actions. Psychologists and scientists break down memory into various types, with each kind of memory having unique attributes and uses dependent on our age, development, maturity, experiences, senses and cognitive abilities. Experiencing trauma, chemical imbalances, drug use and/or Emotional, Physical, Sexual and Narcissistic Abuse can interfere with and have a negative impact on someone's ability to remember or the qualities of those thoughts.

Memories can also be covertly manipulated by a Pathogenic, Character-Disordered Parent who uses Coercive Control, Intermittent Reinforcement, has a malevolent agenda and is skilled at Gaslighting, Blame Shifting and Projection while using repetition, and the support of their regime of loyal enablers, to encourage their Aligned Child(ren) to believe a False Narrative, while suppressing the positive truth. Stockholm Syndrome, Independent Thinker Phenomenon, Psychological Splitting and Black-and-White Thinking also contribute to what a Young/Adult Child remembers. No matter what the reasons, the bottom line is that our memories differ, are imperfect, can fade over time and can be altered or rewritten. Memory and Parental Alienation are both complex phenomena.

While this topic can be deep and has been analyzed in academic/ psychological circles, that wasn't my intent in writing this book. I simply wanted to recount my perspectives of the many memorable and everyday moments that I shared with our children while raising them into adulthood, and when we were in each other's lives. I do believe that as the truth is eventually revealed, righteousness will prevail and we will be back in each other's lives soon.

My heart is and has always been filled with love, compassion, truth, forgiveness, light and goodness. In making the effort to convey my memories and sharing these moments of this mother's **TRUE LOVE** for her children, it is my hope that our son and daughter will know the truth, critically think, research, reflect and remember the many happy times we experienced together.

**I truly love both of our wonderful children with all my heart.**

*"When you look into your mother's eyes,
You know that is the purest love you can find on earth."*

**~Mitch Albom,**

*American Author, Journalist & Musician*

**www.GodCameToMyGarageSale.com**

# AUTHOR BIOGRAPHY

**Dr. Marni Hill Foderaro**, Loving Mother of two wonderful grown children, is both a severely Targeted Mom and an Adult Child Survivor of Parental Alienation. She is also an award-winning educator and the best-selling author of the prominently-endorsed 8-book series: "***TRUE DECEIT FALSE LOVE,***" which creatively addresses and provides tools, terminology and resources for understanding and healing from Parental Alienation and the Intergenerational Family Trauma that comes with surviving familial/marital Domestic Violence and Narcissistic Abuse. This 8th volume: ***"TRUE LOVE: Parental Alienation Cannot Erase the Many Memorable Moments of a Mother's TRUE LOVE For Her Children,"*** includes memories and photo collages to help her son and daughter remember the great times they shared together. Her latest book: "***PARENTAL ALIENATION: quick-read acrostic from an Adult Child Survivor,***" endorsed by Dr. Jennifer J. Harman, Associate Professor, Scientist, world-renowned and Active Researcher of Parental Alienation, gives a concise overview of how children are weaponized and brainwashed by the Pathogenic, Character-Disordered Parent to reject, fear, hate and cut off their Loving, Normal-Range, Targeted Parent. Marni earned her doctorate in education from Northern Illinois University and completed postdoctoral studies at Harvard during a very successful and rewarding 35-year career as a high school special education teacher, with 12 years as a university graduate school adjunct professor. Marni's life was forever changed after experiencing numerous trauma-induced STEs-Spiritually Transformative Encounters. Her 2022 Hollywood Book Fest runner-up, 2020 Best Books finalist Award Winning and 5-Star Reader's Favorite Spiritual fiction, inspired by true events: ***"God Came To My Garage Sale"*** is prominently endorsed by James Redfield, best-selling author of "*The Celestine Prophecy*" series of books and other notables in the Spiritual community, including founding directors of IANDS-International Association for Near Death Studies. In addition to her TV/podcast interviews, speaking engagements and various writing endeavors, Marni is a contributing author to numerous anthology books. In 2022 Dr. Marni Hill Foderaro was inducted into the Bestselling Authors International (BAI) Organization. Marni was born in the South, raised her children in the Midwest and lives in the Caribbean. She is a lover of animals, nature, music and world travel who handles life's challenges with love, compassion, forgiveness and positivity. She values honesty, integrity, equality and goodness and prays for peace on earth and understanding within our families. Marni believes that truth eventually prevails over lies, and that no Young/Adult Child deserves to experience the extreme Child Abuse of Parental Alienation.

*"As long as we have memories, yesterday remains.*
*As long as we have hope, tomorrow awaits.*
*As long as we have LOVE, today is beautiful."*

**~ Abhishek Shukla,**

*Author, Doctor & Influencer*

---

*"Memory is a way of holding on to the things you love,*
*the things you are, the things you never want to lose."*

**~ Kevin Arnold,**

*Teenage Character from "The Wonder Years" played by Actor Fred Savage*

---

*"Memory is the treasury and guardian of all things."*

**~ Cicero,**

*Roman Statesman, Scholar, Philosopher & Writer*

*"Life isn't a matter of milestones, but of moments."*
**~ Rose Kennedy,**
*American Philanthropist & Matriarch*

---

*"Memory is the diary that we all carry about with us."*
**~ Oscar Wilde,**
*Irish Author, Poet & Playwright*

---

*"Reserve your memories, keep them well,
what you forget, you can never retell."*
**~ Louisa May Alcott,**
*American Novelist, Short Story Writer & Poet*

*"Without memory, there is no healing.*

*Without forgiveness there is no future."*
**~ Desmond Tutu,**
*South African Bishop & Human Rights Activist*

* * * *

*"Sometimes we can't let go of memories because they are constant reminders of a great story that we never expected to end."*
**~ Shashi Prakash,**
*Author, Dreamer & Good Listener*

* * * *

*"I find out more and more every day how important it is for people to share their memories."*
**~ Mister Fred Rogers,**
*American Children's TV Host, Author & Minister*

*"Our memories are our truths only because of the meaning and filters we give to them. The way we view our past very literally determines how we live today."*

**~ Luisa Carel,**

*Passion Harvest International Ambassador & Podcaster*

---  * * * * ---

*"It takes one thought, one second, one moment or positive memory to act as a catalyst for the light to gradually seep in again."*

**~ Fearne Cotton,**

*English Author & Broadcaster*

---  * * * * ---

*"Memory is the treasure house of the mind wherein the monuments thereof are kept and preserved."*

**~ Thomas Fuller,**

*17th Century English Historian, Clergyman, Doctor & Writer*

*"If I had a box just for wishes and
dreams that had never come true.
The box would be empty, except for the memory of
how they were answered by you."*

**~ *Jim Croce*,**

*American Singer-Songwriter*

---   ✶ ✶ ✸ ✶ ✶   ---

*"We didn't realize we were making memories;
we just knew we were having fun."*

**~ Winnie the Pooh,**

*Good-Natured Bear Character,
Created by English Author & Illustrator A.A. Milne*

# MOM'S MANY MEMORABLE MOMENTS

My 8th TDFL volume:

***TRUE LOVE***

***Parental Alienation Cannot Erase the
Many Memorable Moments of a Mother's
TRUE LOVE For Her Children***

is this loving mom's attempt to help jog the memory of our two beautiful children.

-ABC Song From The Jackson 5 Musical Group

-ABCs Learning Our Letters With A Song

-ABCs Practicing Writing Capital And Lower Case Letters on Manilla Paper That Had Dotted Lines

-A Light In The Attic Shel Silverstein Book

-Acapulco-Family Vacation

-Acne Angst

-Acrostic Poetry Writing

-Action Figures-Batman

-Action, For Movie Acting To Start, But I Would Always Then Say Figures

-Adler Planetarium-Chicago-Space Ice Cream Food

-Advent Calendars With Chocolates

-Air Heads Candies

-Air Jordans, Baby Sports Shoes

-Air Show-US Air Force Thunderbirds, Mother's Day In Fort Lauderdale, Florida

-Airplane Wing Pins From Pilots We Would Get When We Flew On Airplanes For Our Vacations Or Trips

-Aladdin Movie

-Aladdin Song, A Whole New World

-Alarm Clock-Hitting The Snooze Button

-All Dogs Go To Heaven Movie

-Allergy Testing And Shots

-Alligator Feeding In Florida

-Allowance or No Allowance, Just The $5 Song Game

-Almond Joy Candy Bars Sometimes You Feel Like A Nut

-Alpaca Farm-Barrington

-Altoids Mints In Metal Can

-Alvechurch, England Where Grandad And Grandma Lived -Always There For You

-Ambrosia Bakery Cakes, Euro American Patisserie

-Amusement Park Rides

-Angels

-Animal Crackers

-Animal Welfare

-Ant Farms

-Antique Stores Road Trip Searching For Old Treasures

-Apartment-Mom Helping Set Up And Clean

-Apple Cider

-Apple Crisp

-Apple Picking

-Apple Pie Ala Mode

-Aquarium-Shedd In Downtown Chicago

-Archeology Interest, Discovering The Past

-Archery

-Architecture Tour Chicago River

-Ariana Grande Concert Surprise On Florida College Visit Trip

-Arlington Heights Metropolis Theatre Plays And Musicals

-Art And Clay Classes

-Art Institute Of Chicago

-Art Projects With Mom

-Arthur Theme Song, Hey, What A Wonderful Kind Of Day

-Arthur TV Show

-Asleep or Faking Like You're Asleep, Until You Smile

-Asthma Plan

-Astronaut Dehydrated Food And Ice Cream

-Assignment Red Books

-Audiologist-Loss Of Hearing As A Toddler

-Australian Shepherd Dogs-Hoosier, Wanabe, Ceydee, Bella

-Avocado-Growing Seeds In Water With Toothpicks

-Avon Skin-So-Soft For Mosquito Bites

-Awards, Accomplishments And Achievements

-Aziz Anzari Comedian Show In Chicago And Poster, Mom Surprised Me

-BLT Sandwiches-Bacon, Lettuce And Tomato

-BRAT Diet-Banana, Rice, Apple Sauce And Tea

-Baby Books Where Mom Documented Our Childhoods

-Baby Calendar Where Mom Wrote What We Did Daily

-Baby Clothes, We Always Looked So Cute

-Baby Spare Ribs Nickname

-Back Street Boys Boy Band

-Back To The Future Movies-Time Travel Are Mom's Favorite Movies

-Back Yard Hammock For Two

-Back Yard Hot Tub, So Much Fun Soaking Out In Nature

-Back Yard Overnight Camping

-Back Yard Pink Play House

-Back Yard Playing

-Back Yard Swing

-Backpack Key Chains, Many Types Including Figment

-Backstreet Boys Musical Group

-Bahai Temple-Wilmette, Illinois Landmark

-Baked Potatoes Loaded With Bacon, Cheddar Cheese And Sour Cream

-Baking Soda Paste For Bug Bites

-Ballet Class With Pink Tutu Outfit In Barrington, Illinois

-Ballet-Nutcracker Christmas Show In Chicago

-Balloon Bouquets

-Balloons

-Banana Splits With Whipped Cream And Sprinkles, In Our Special Yellow Ceramic Banana Boat Bowls, Mom Had Those When She Was A Child

-Bandaids-Colorful, Sesame Street, Barney

-Bank Taking You To Chase To Open Up Your Own Account With No Cosigner

-Barnes And Noble-Friday Nights At The Kid's Section

-Barney-The Purple Dinosaur TV Show

-Barrel of Monkeys Game

-Barrington Day Care

-Barrington High School (Broncos)

-Barrington Original Tracks-Fast Food And French Fries

-Barrington Montessori Pre-School, Such Nice Teachers

-BASA-Barrington Area Soccer Association

-Baseball Cards

-Baseball-Catcher

-Baseball Games-Snacks At Concessions

-Baseball Leagues And Tournaments

-Basketball, Play Horse, Shorten Letters To Play "OX"

-Basketball Leagues

-Bass Pro Shops

-Bat Trapped In The House

-Bathtime Fizzy Balls Soap And Washable Bath Paint

-Bathtub Paints

-Batman Bat Cave, We Had All The Accessories And Action Figures

-Batman Movie Series

-Batman Song By Seal, Kiss From A Rose

-Batman's Cape, Mom Made Many Capes

-Bazooka Bubble Gum With Messages

-Beach-Lake Forest, Illinois

-Beach-Mexico With Black/White Photos And Striped Shirts

-Bead Necklaces

-Beaded Socks To Match Outfits

-Bean-Chicago Cloud Gate

-Beanie Baby Bears

-Beatrix Potter Peter Rabbit

-Beatrix Potter Themed Nursery

-Beauty And The Beast Movie

-Bed, Bath And Beyond Stores

-Bedknobs And Broomsticks Movie

-Bedrooms

-Bedtime Stories-Curling Up And Reading With Mom

-Bee Stings-Mom Getting The Stinger Out

-Beef Stew And Veggies In The Crockpot

-Beese Park Mom Took Us For Soccer Games And Kite Flying Events

-Before Care St. Anne's Extended Care

-Belgium Baseball Trip, Bruges, Bringing Trinkets To Trade

-Belgium Waffles, Special Ones Made For Christmas Morning

-Bell Ringing When Sick, Then Mom Would Come And Make Us Feel Better

-Belly Dancer At Epcot's Moroccan Restaurant

-Belly Farts-Blow Then Laughing Uncontrollably

-Benjamin Buttons Movie-The Curious Case of-Mom Cried In The Movie Theatre, Even After Everyone Had Left

-Berenstain Bears Stories, Such A Cute Bear Family

-Beta Fish-Blue And Red From Ricky's Pet Shop Barrington

-Bible, Mom Always Bought Us A Special Bible

-Big Bird, Sesame Street TV

-Big Book Of Paper Airplanes

-Bike Parades In Our Victoria Woods Neighborhood

-Bike Rides

-Bikes, Training Wheels, Then Getting Our First Two-Wheelers

-Bill Nye The Science Guy TV Show

-Bingo Games And Winning Prizes

-Bird Feeders In Our Backyard

-Bird Seed Balls-Popcorn And Peanut Butter

-Birth

-Birthday Gifts-$25 Single Dollar Bills Rolled

-Birthday Parties, Big Celebrations With Friends And Neighbors

-Birthdays

-Birthstones-Amethyst And Garnet, Parents Were Sapphires

-Black Lights

-Black Stallion Movie

-Blackbird Song Guitar Intro

-Blackhawks Hockey Tickets-Surprise, Christmas, Denver

-Blanket Forts And Flashlights

-Blizzards From Dairy Queen

-Bloomin' Onion Outback Steakhouse-Crystal Lake, Illinois

-Blowing Bubbles

-Blue Dog-Mom's Childhood Stuffed Animal She Had All Her Life

-Blue Moon Brunch-LBTS-Lauderdale By The Sea, All-You-Can-Eat Seafood Buffet With Peel Your Own Shrimp And Crab Legs

-Blueberry Bushes In Our Front Yard

-Blueberry Pancakes

-Boats, Up High At Marine Store On The Way To Long Lake

-Bob The Seagull Joined Us On Every Trip No Matter Where We Were, Now On Arm Tattoo

-Bobbing For Apples In October For Fall Fest And Halloween

-Bolos From Tennessee, Cool, Rustic Cowboy Necklaces

-Boogie Boards-Maine And Mexico

-Book Fairs (Scholastic) List To Pick Out Books And We Would Always Donate Money Or Books For Others

-Books

-Boots-Splash In Puddles While It Was Raining

-Bop It Game, We Always Had Such Fun Games To Play

-Botanic Gardens-Glencoe, Illinois, Play In Fountains

-Bouncy Balls

-Bouncy Houses At Birthday Parties

-Bowls And Cups With Straws

-Boxes-Make The Best Forts

-Braces-Night Guard, Retainer, Walk Across From St. Anne's School To The Orthodontist

-Braided Hair

-Braids-In Hair In Acapulco, Mexico

-Breadmaker, Kids Would Love To Make Homemade Bread, Put All The Ingredients In, Crack An Egg, Add The Yeast And Press The Timer Button

-Brookfield Zoo-Tram Ride To See All Of The Animals

-Brownies Girl Scouts

-Brownies Chocolate With Whipped Cream And Sprinkles

-Broyhill Distressed Furniture In Our Living Room

-Bubble Baths-Mr. Bubble, Bathtime Was Always So Much Fun

-Bubble Baths With Action Figures And Toys

-Bubble Gum-Bazooka, It Always Had A Fun Comic To Read

-Bubble Gum Machines

-Buc-ees Gas Stations In Tennessee, Getting Lots Of Souvenirs

-Bucket Game-Homemade Bozo's Circus

-Buckingham Fountain-Grant Park, Chicago

-Buckingham Palace-London, England

-Buehler YMCA In Palatine, Illinois For Swim Lessons And Rock Climbing And Days Off Of School Programs

-Buffalo Grove Apartment, Watching Your Sister's UNE College Graduation On The TV Livestream

-Buffalo Wild Wings-Garlic Parmesan

-Bug Catching Jars

-Bugles Snacks-Put On Fingers To Make Long Nails

-Bugs Life Disney Movie And Multi-Sensory Experience

-Building Blocks To Make Forts And Buildings

-Bull Fight Mexico. Left Early When We Saw What It Was About

-Bull's Games To Watch Michael Jordan And Eat At The Concession Stands

-Bumper Cars

-Bungie Jumping-Great America

-Bunk Beds

-Buried Treasures-Using Professional Metal Detector

-Burrs-On Hikes, Like Velcro, Picking The Prickers Off Our Jeans

-Busse Woods-Canoeing In Schaumburg

-Butt Dial Blessing And Reconnection

-Butter Making-Shaking Baby Jars Of Cream

-Butterfly Garden Sign-Art Project With Mini Tiles

-Butterfly Home Kit-Insect Lore With Live Caterpillars/Chrysalises

-CDs

-Cabbage Patch Kids

-Cakes Ambrosia Fancy Expensive Cakes And Costco Sheet Cakes

-Calendars And Schedules, Mom Would Help Us Stay Organized

-Camp Eberhart, Three Rivers Michigan Riflery And Water Skiing, Mom Mailed Me A Camp Fill-In-The-Blank Letter Everyday When I Was At Camp For Two Weeks

-Camping At Home

-Candles At Night At Dinner

-Candy

-Candy Canes, On Christmas Tree And Huge One In Stockings

-Candy Stores

-Candyland Board Game

-Canoeing

-Canopy Crib- Painted Nursery Furniture

-Car Rides To Go To Sleep

-Caramel Apples

-Carebears Stuffed Animals

-Carefree

-Carl's Christmas-Big Black Dog Adventure Books With No Words

-Carving Pumpkin Faces

-Cartwheels

-Carwash Fast Eddie's, Watching The Washers From Inside The Car

-Casper The Friendly Ghost Show

-Casseroles For Dinner

-Cassette Tapes And Cassette Tape Player

-Castle Lego Game-Knights And Cannons

-Casts On Ankle And Wrist, Friends Would Sign

-Cat Baby Miracle Who Was Born In Our Pink Playhouse In The Backyard

-Cat House For Maxie Made By Mom's Students At LEAP

-Cat Memorial Garden For Maxie And Midnight In Side Yard

-Catchpenny Resale Store, Downtown Barrington

-Caterpillar Yellow Riding Toy, Light Up, Made Noise

-Caterpillars, Watching Them Grow Into Butterflies

-Catlow Theatre-Barrington, Great Buttered Popcorn, Very Tiny Bathroom

-Caves-Bats, Cold And Wet

-Ceiling Fan Watch To Fall Asleep

-Ceiling Glow Stickers

-Cello In Music Room

-Cemetery

-Cereal-Lucky Charms With Marshmallows, Magically Delicious

-Chain O'Lakes

-Chalk Drawings On The Sidewalk In Victoria Woods

-Champion Ring-Notes From Friends For Birthday

-Change Drawer By Front Door For Ice Cream Truck

-Charlie Brown's Christmas TV Show

-Charlie Brown's Pumpkin Patch

-Charlotte's Web Book by E.B. White And Movie

-Charm Bracelet-Hearts From 1ˢᵗ Year

-Checkers-Oversized, Red And Black, Big Rug Mat

-Cheese Curds-Culvers; Girl Scout Volunteer Serving Event

-Cheesy Fries

-Chef Outfit To Dress Up When Cooking

-Chessies At The Ice House, Train Restaurant-Barrington

-Chewable Vitamins, Shapes

-Chia Pets-Growing Alfalfa Sprouts

-Chicago Bears At Soldier Field

-Chicago Blackhawks At United Center

-Chicago Bulls Dream Team United Center

-Chicago Care Bags-Magnificent Mile-Mom Helping Homeless

-Chicago Children's Museum

-Chicago Civic Orchestra-Mom Took Us To Free Concerts

-Chicago History Museum

-Chicka-Chicka Boom Boom Book

-Chicken Hatchlings-At Chicago Science And Industry Museum And At School

-Chicken Noodle Soup With Crackers

-Chicken Pot Pies

-Children's Bible-Reading Verses And Reflecting And Relating

-Children's Museums

-Children's Theater-In Play As An Animal; Another Play I Was A Dragon Who Was Slayed In The First Scene, So I Stayed On The Floor The Entire Play

-Chinatown-Live Frog Legs Cut Off And Sold

-Chitty Chitty Bang Bang Movie-("Remarkable Weather We Are Having For This Time Of Year, Do You Not Think So?"…"I Want That Car")

-Chocolate Chip Cookies-Eating Cookie Dough

-Chocolate Dipped Ice Cream Cones From Dairy Queen

-Chocolate Easter Bunnies

-Chocolate Milk

-Chocolate Shakes

-Choo-Choo Restaurant-Des Plaines-Food Comes On A Track

-Chores-Mom Always Gave Us Responsibilities To Be Responsible And Learn To Be Independent

-Christmas Cards-Brother-Sister Photo Greetings Each Year

-Christmas Caroling

-Christmas Eve-Going To a Movie, Then Midnight Mass

-Christmas Lights-Driving Around In Jammies With Blankets

-Christmas Morning Waking Up To See Presents Under The Tree

-Christmas Pickle Hidden In The Christmas Tree

-Christmas Stockings, Personalized Needlepoint From Land's End

-Chuck E. Cheese Tickets, Show, Climbing, Balls, Pizza, Where A Kid Can Be A Kid

-Cider Donuts From Quig's Apple Orchard In Mundelein, IL

-Cinderella Dress-Up Toy Plastic Slipper High Heels

-Cinderella Movie

-Cinnamon Sugar Toast With Butter

-Circus

-Civic Opera House Free Concerts Chicago Across From Art Institute, Sitting Up Close See Instruments, Taking The Train There

-Clay Projects

-Clay Monet Painting Figurines In Lake Zurich

-Clifford The Big Red Dog Book And TV Show

-Climbing Ladders

-Climbing Trees

-Closet Thing From Creating The Leprechaun Book

-Clothing Tags-Mom Cutting Them All Off So They Are Not Itchy

-Clouds, Figuring Out Their Shapes

-Cocomotion-Hot Chocolate Maker, Our Special Kitchen Appliance

-Cody Bear-My Favorite Stuffed Animal I Got When I Was Two Years Old, Took Him On A Train Ride-But Lost Him At O'Hare Airport-Mom Went Back For Years To Try And Find Him

-Coin Collection With Money From All Over The World

-Coin Drawer in Dresser By The Front Door, Used For Ice Cream Truck

-Coin Riding Horse Outside Of Stores

-Collages Made With Photos And Glued Magazine Images

-College Visits In Florida, Even Went To Jacksonville University

-Colorado Family Road Trip

-Colorado Skiing And Snowboarding With Mom At Winter Park

-Colored Pencils

-Colorforms-Thin Vinyl Sheets With Designs To Create A Collage

-Coloring Books For Children And Adults

-Comfy Couch Dust Bunnies Named Fuzzy And Wuzzy -Ten Second Tidy Show With Girl-Clown Named Loonette And Her Doll Molly

-Communion Big Cannoli Cake With Small Cannolis Inside

-Computers and Electronics P52, P53, X-Box, X-Box 360, Games

-Confirmation Classes At St. Theresa's In Palatine, Illinois

-Confirmation Ceremony

-Concession Stands

-Connect The Dots Board Game

-Construction Paper Art Projects

-Cookie Cutters, So Many Shapes, Baked With Sprinkles

-Cookie Jar Kits

-Cookies Tollhouse Chocolate Chip, Oatmeal Raisin, Peanut Butter

-Cooking Classes. Chef's Hat And Apron

-Corn Mazes At Pumpkin Farms

-Corn On The Cob, In Corn Shaped Plates, With Cool Corn-Shaped Holders On The Ends

-Cornerstones Montessori Home Care Preschool

-Corvette Sweatshirt-McCormick Place Chicago Auto Show, I Loved Red Corvettes

-Cosmic Bowling Bumpers, Bowl In The Dark With Neon Lights

-Costa Rica Trips, Mom Paid For Them

-Costco Lunch And Buy In Bulk

-Cotton Candy, Favorite Special Treat At Fairs

-Coupon Book Homemade For Mom-Free Hugs

-Coupon Cutting And Collecting

-Cowboy Hat From River Ranch, Florida, Christmas Trip With Mom

-Crab Leg Cracking Trick

-Cracker Barrel Restaurants, Stopped At A Few When Mom Flew To Oklahoma To Save Me And We Both Drove Back To Palatine, Illinois

-Cracker Jacks Toy Inside

-Crafts

-Cranberries Song

-Crawlspace In Basement, Climbing Up

-Crayons Melting On Glass Bottle For Candle Holders

-Crawfish In Front Victoria Woods House Landscaping For Two Years

-Crayola Crayons, Pencils And Markers

-Creepy Crawlers Machine; Mom Also Had One As Child-And Flower Power

-Creme Brûlée Desserts, Cookbook

-Crepe Paper Flowers Pipe Cleaners

-Crocs Slip On Clogs With Many Personalized Pin Jibbutz Charm Accessories

-Cross Above Bedroom Door

-Crossword Puzzles

-Cruise Trips

-Crystals

-Cub Games At Chicago's Wrigley Field

-Cube Game Boy, Wii, DS Or PSP, Intendo

-Culvers Cheese Curds-Girl Scouts Event, Serving Customers

-Cupcakes and Licking Batter Off The Mixers

-Curious George Books, Movies And Stuffed Animal

-Curly Straws, Fun To Watch Milk Go Up When Sipping

-Cursive, Learning How To Write And Connect Letters

-Cursive Practice Books

-Cutie Pie, Mom Would Always Call Me That

-Cutting Crusts Off Of Sandwiches, Especially PBJ's

-D And J Bistro Lake Zurich Fancy French Restaurant In Lake Zurich, Illinois

-Daffodils, So Pretty In The Garden, Grown In Bunches

-Dairy Queen Blizzards. Shakes With Candy

-Dairy Queen Vanilla Cone Dipped In Chocolate

-Daisy Girl Scouts

-Dalmatians 101 Book And Movie, My Tail Is Cold

-Dan In Real Life-One of Mom's Favorite Movies With Steve Carell

-Dance Mat DDR "Stay Cool"

-Dances At School Sock Hop Disco Balls Decorations Outfits

-Dancing On Tables to Michael Jordan's Space Jam And I Believe I Can Fly, Video Is Still On Mom's Phone And Makes Her Laugh

-Dave And Busters Winning Tickets And Arcade Games

-Daytona International Speedway-Christmas 2023 Road Trip With Mom, 3 Laps, 157.4 MPH

-Decorated Tennis Shoes With Markers

-Decorating Our House For Holidays

-Deep End Of The Swimming Pool

-Dentist's Charlie The Water Suction

-Desserts First

-Devil's Head Wisconsin Ski And Snowboard Family Trip

-Diamonds, Mom Passed Down From Family Inheritance

-Didier Pumpkin Patch And Farm In Buffalo Grove, Illinois

-Dill Pickles And Drinking Pickle Juice

-Diners For Hot Dogs, Hamburgers, Fries And Milkshakes

-Dining Room Never Used For Dinner, Mom Wanted To Use Special China Plates 1x/Week, But Nobody Else In Family Wanted To

-Dinosaurs

-Dioramas, Making Nature Scenes In Shoe Boxes

-Disco Balls Dances At School

-Discovering, Exploring, Curiosity

-Discovery Zone, Play Place Like Chuck-E-Cheese

-Disney Trips, Florida And California

-District 211, Mom Taught At Palatine High School And LEAP

-Diving Boards Doing Flips

-Diving Off The High Dive At The Barrington Park District Pool

-Dodgeball Games

-Dog Rescue-White Dog In Busy Road-Mom Rescued And Got Him In There Car And Called Owner

-Dollar Store Shopping

-Dolls-We Liked Stuffed Animals And Action Figures Instead

-Dolphins, Mexico Experience, Got To Pet And Kiss

-Dominican Republic All-Inclusive Vacation With Mom, Held Snake, Birds, Played Volleyball, Fascinated By The Food Art Displays

-Donate, We Were Always Sharing With Others

-Donating Our Toys, Books And Clothes

-Donley's Wild Wild West In Union, Panning For Gold, Watching A Cowboy Shootout, Learning To Lasso

-Double Baked Potatoes With Bacon, Cheddar Cheese, Butter And Sour Cream

-Double Bubble Bubble Gum

-Double Choc(olate) Frap(uccino) From Starbuck's

-Dr. Seuss Books Theodore Giesel The Cat In The Hat Thing One Thing Two WHO-Ville (Horton Hears A Who Book)

-Dragon in Play, Was Slayed At Beginning And Spent Entire Play On The Floor. Very Funny

-Driver's License Went To McHenry 2x, Easier Less Traffic

-Drum Set

-Duck Duck Goose Sitting And Running Around The Circle Game

-Duck Sounds With Hands

-Dude Ranch

-Dumbo The Flying Baby Elephant Cartoon

-Dunkin Donuts French Crullers, Jelly Filled, Rainbow Sprinkles

-Dying Easter Eggs And Sometimes Using Glitter

-ESPN Zone

-ET Movie, Phone Home

-Ear Infections, Mom Told Doctor Too Many Antibiotic Medicines

-Ear Muffs

-Ear Tube Surgery

-Earth From Above Photos Display At Millennium Park, Book Was Expensive

-Easter Baskets White Chocolate Cross, Jelly Beans, Malted Chocolate Eggs, Easter Toys, One Golden Egg Filled With Money

-Easter Bunny At The Foundry In Barrington

-Easter Egg Hunt In Arlington Heights, Illinois Public Pool, Collecting Floating Plastic Easter Eggs In The Water

-Easter Egg Hunts In Our Backyard, And At River Front Park In Fox River Grove

-Easton, Maryland To Visit Grandparents

-Easy Bake Oven, Making Mini Cakes With Frosting

-Eating Snow, White Not Yellow

-Edible Fruit Arrangements And Bouquets

-Editing, Mom Would Always Correct The Grammar And Punctuation Of Our Papers And Reports Before We Would Turn Them In

-Egg Harbor Cafe Fresh Orange Juice Coloring Contests

-Egg-In-A-Hole

-Egg Salad Sandwiches

-Eggnog With Sprinkles

-Eggrolls Mom Made

-Eiffel Tower Climbing Stairs To Top In Paris France, And NO, Mom Did Not Get Lost, That Was A Made-Up Story

-Elder Bug Invasion In Our Backyard By The Hot Tub

-Electric Bill At Knolls In Nashville And Executive Manor Apartments In Fort Lauderdale Paid By Mom

-Electric Guitar, Mom Got A New One After I Stole Hers

-Elevator Buttons, We Always Liked To Press The Button And Jump Just Before The Elevator Reached Our Floor

-Elf On A Shelf Book And Figurine

-Elmhurst College Soccer Overnight Camp Look Out Window Field Dorm At Elmhurst College For Soccer Camp, Broke Wrist Bright Lime Green Cast

-Elmo, Red Sesame Street Character

-Embassy Suites Deerfield, Illinois With Grandparents From England

-Empathy Some Don't Have It

-England Trips Alvechurch, London

-English Muffin Pizzas

-English Pram Baby Buggy. Once Didn't Have On Brakes And It Rolled Down the Driveway With You In It. Mom Sprinted Faster Than She Ever Did And Stopped It Just Before It Hit The Curb

-Epcot Disney World Countries

-Epcot Disney Fireworks

-Epcot Disney Italy T-Shirt

-Epcot Disney Resort Hotels

-Etch-A-Sketch With Twisty Knobs To Make Designs

-Evanston Hospital-Where Our Son Was Born By C-Section

-Everglades Florida Feeding Gators

-Everyday Events

-Executive Manor Apartments-Fort Lauderdale, Florida

-Eye Glasses

33

-F.R.G. Library Bags with Patches Lifetime Member, Names On Shelf

-F.R.G. Rec (Recreation) Council Soccer And Baseball

-Fake Blue Bird Egg Put In Nest, Fooled Mom

-Falling Asleep In Food When I Was In My High Chair

-Falling Up Shel Silverstein Black And White Book

-Family Calendar Mom Kept Up To Date With All Of Our Activities

-Fantasia Movie With Mickey Mouse, Made Me Sleepy

-Farmer's Market-Barrington Cruise Night Thursdays

-Farms

-Fawn-Baby Deer In The Front Yard

-Ferris Wheel Amusement Park Rides

-Feta Cheese And Kalamata Olives In Greek Salads

-Field Museum Chicago

-Fifties Sock Hop Dances At St. Anne's

-Figment Imagination Purple Dragon From Disney

-Figment Key Chain-Kept Promise To Use In With First Car Keys

-Fire Drill Go Outside of House And Meet Up As A Family

-Fire Fly Catching At Night Putting Them In Mason Jars With Holes In Top

-Fireplace

-Fireworks Foundry Stay In Car-Mosquitos

-First Snow In The Woods Photographic Deer Book

-Fish Art Project We Made For Our Upstairs Kids' Bathroom Around The Mirror

-Fish Tank With Bright Colored Pebbles

-Five Dollar Challenge, Name That Musical Artist Game

-Flag Football

-Flamingo Gardens in Davie, FL For Mother's Day

-Flamingos At The Zoo

-Flashlight Tag Outside In The Neighborhood

-Fleece Blankets Ties Vegas Made For Grandparents And For On Angels Wings-Gold Award, Making Fleece Paw-Print Blankets

-Florida Christmas Road Trip

-Florida College Visits

-Florida Move To Fort Lauderdale

-Flower Pressing

-Focus Karate Classes

-Folding Clothes With Mom

-Folding Towels

-Fooseball-Loseball

-Football Rose Ceremony

-Football Stickers

-Footprints In The Sand

-Footy Pajamas Zip Up Fleece

-Forest Knoll Townhome In Palatine-Cartwheels When Rick Showed Us The Apartment Mom Would Move To

-Forest Preserve Bike Rides And Picnics

-Fort Lauderdale Drive Old Truck-Gifted with New Truck

-Fortune Cookies From Chinese Restaurants

-Four Leaf Clovers

-Fox And Hound Movie

-Fox In Our Backyard

-Fox River Grove, Illinois

-Fox River Grove Library Lifetime Members. Shelf With Name

-Foyer Decor For Every Holiday

-Frank Lloyd Wright Houses Studio In Oak Park, Illinois Architecture

-French Dip Sandwiches Mom Would Make

-French Fries Super-Sized From McDonalds

-French Toast-Mom Would Add Cinnamon And Vanilla-I Would Always Want Mom To Cut It, Even When I Could Cut It Myself

-Fried Rice Mom Made

-Fried Wontons

-Friendship Bracelets To Make And Give To Others

-Frog In The Garage

-Frontier Truck After Tacoma Truck-Both Gifts 100% Paid For From Rick And Mom

-Frosty Shakes From Wendy's

-Frosty The Snowman Book And Movie

-Frozen Pizzas

-Frozen Waffles, Mom Would Heat Up The Maple Syrup

-Fruit Roll-Ups

-Fudge From Long Grove

-Fudgesicles

-Fun Balls McDonalds-Chuck-E-Cheese-Even Had A Small Pool With Fun Balls At Home

-Fun Dips Candy Valentines

-Fun, Mom Always Wanted Us To Have Fun And Enjoy Life

-Furniture Moving-Mom Paid Movers

-Furniture Painting

-Fuzzy Socks

-Gak Splat Nickelodeon

-Galatis Pasta Dinners, Watching The Train Go By

-Gameboy Left At The Chicago O'Hare Airport

-Games

-Garage Sales

-Garden Flags

-Gardens, Mom Made Our Yard Look Beautiful

-Garden Statues-Angel And Boy With No Hand Who Is Reading Book, We Secretly Buried His Hand In The Garden So Mom Wouldn't Know

-Garfield Drawings, Mom Would Always Teach Kids To Draw

-Garfield The Cat Show

-Gargling Learning How To Gargle

-Garlands In Barrington Retirement Home For Fancy High Tea

-Gatlinburg Christmas Travel Plans

-Gatorade Popsicle Invention (G. Sports Science Institute-Bar)

-Gazebo In Backyard To Chill And Open Easter Baskets

-Gazebo Grill Dinner In F.R.G.

-Gecko (Feeding Him Grasshoppers)

-Geisha Girl Halloween Costume

-Genie In A Bottle

-Getting Glasses For Reading/Distance

-Ghost Kleenex Hanging Decorations

-Ghostbusters Movie. Who Ya Gonna Call?

-Gift Of The Sea Book By Anne Morrow Lindbergh Shells Chapters, Mom's Favorite Author

-Gilmore Girls TV Series Watching Together On The Couch

-Gingerbread Houses, Put Together With Icing And Decorate With Gumdrops And Candy Canes

-Girl Scout Awards Gold, Silver And Bronze

-Girl Scout Patches

-Girl Scout Trips To Lucerne, Switzerland And Savannah, Georgia That Mom Paid For

-Girl Scout Vests

-Girl Scouts

-Giving Tree Book By Shel Silverstein

-Glasses

-Glitter Art Projects

-Globes Made With Special Stones

-Go-Carts

-Go Fish Card Game

-Goat Milking

-Gobstoppers Willy Wonka Candy

-Goebbert's Farm In South Barrington For Pumpkins

-Going With Mom To Plays And Musicals

-Gold CRV And Van, And Black MDX, The Mom Mobiles

-Golden Egg Veruka Salt Willy Wonka Easter Egg Hunts, "I Want A Goose That Lays Golden Eggs For Easter, I Want It Now."

-Go Carts

-Goldfish Winning With Ping Pong Balls In Bowls Of Water From Carnivals

-Goldilocks And The Three Bears

-Good Dog Carl Book With No Words

-Good Luck Charms

-Good Shepherd Hospital, Where Our Daughter Was Born, Barrington, Illinois

-Goodbye Earl By Dixie Chicks, Maryann And Wanda Were The Best Of Friends, Knew All The Words, Cut A Demo-Tape At Great America 6-Flags Amusement Park

-Goodnight Moon Book

-Goodwill Thrift Store-Getting Deals On Gently-Used Clothes And Housewares

-Goosebumps Book Series

-Goosebumps Show

-Graffiti Wall In Bedroom

-Grand Canyon Trip, Short Visit Out West

-Grand Piano, In Our Music Room, So Beautiful

-Grand Slam, Mom Was So Happy, Dad Corrected My Swing Stance

-Grandma Moses Folk Artist Later In Life-Mom Took Me To Lyric Opera, Cloris Leachman One Woman Show

-Grandparent's Cards And Gifts And Visits

-Grant Park Chicago Buckingham Fountain Festivals

-Great America 6-Flags In Gurnee (Mom Did A Bungee Jump)

-Great Books, Classics From Barnes And Noble

-Great Wolf Lodge Waterpark And Tube Slides

-Greek Costume, Uncle's Childhood Evzoni Outfit

-Greek Food, Mom's Favorite

-Greek Taverna Restaurant At Lauderdale-By-The-Sea

-Greektown Halsted Street, Chicago, Illinois, Went To The Greek Isles And The Santorini Restaurant

-Green Garden Chinese Food

-Grilled Cheese Sandwiches With Tomato Soup

-Grinch Who Stole Christmas

-Groceries Delivered From Sprouts In Nashville

-Grocery Shopping With Mom, Riding In The Cart

-Groin Pain, Unexplained For Years, Doctors/Specialists Could Not Find Cause

-Guess How Much I Love You? Book With A Rabbit

-Guess That Musical Artist $5 Game

-Guitar Hero Legends Of Rock Jukebox Hero

-Guitar Lessons

-Guitar Songs Tom Dooley And Blackbird

-Gymboree Matching Colorful Outfits

-Gymnastics Buehler YMCA

-Gyros Greek Shaved Meat From A Spit, With Tzatziki Yogurt And Cucumber Sauce

-Haiku Poetry Writing

-Hair Ribbons

-Haircuts

-Half-Time Shows And Snacks

-Hall Of Fame Family Road Trip

-Hall Of The Troll King Magical Music Box Stories British Magazine Gift From Grandparents To Introduce Us To Classical Music Which Was Played In The Background, Scary Story When Two Kids Went Into a Mountain

-Halloween Candy

-Halloween Decorating Front Porch With White Cobwebs

-Halloween Hob Goblin For The Front Door Window

-Halloween Make-Up And Fake Blood Dripping Out Of Our Mouths

-Halloween Skeleton Came To Our House Every Year (Who Was Actually Mom)

-Hammering Nails In Wood

-Hammock Backyard

-Hamster Pets From Ricky's Pet Shop

-Hand Sculptures Thumbs Up-Peace

-Hand Stands

-Handprint Sweatshirts

-Happy Meal Toys McDonalds

-Harold and the Purple Crayon Book

-Harper Animal Hospital-Mom Coming To Work With Me, She Was Always Mopping and Doing Laundry While I Walked The Dogs

-Harriet Tubman and The Underground Railroad Toy Set, Did Report

-Harper Graduation Scrapbook And Photo Reprints For Dad, Babysitter And Friends, Mom Made Even Though She Was Not Invited And Watched Ceremony On Livestream From Her Apartment One Mile Away

-Harry Potter Books and Collecting The Series

-Haunted House In Lake Zurich And Fox River Grove

-Hawthorn/Westgate Mall In Vernon Hills, Illinois

-Hay Rides At Fall Pumpkin Patches

-Head Stands

-Headgear For Braces

-Heart Band Guitar Intro, Mom's $1,000 Challenge, A Challenge That Is Still Open

-Heart Ring Handmade In BHS Jewelry Class, Gave To Mom

-Heating Pads to Warm Up

-Heelies-Skating Through The Louvre Museum in Paris, France

-Helicopter Rides

-Helmets

-Helping The Homeless With Food And Buying a Sweater

-Henna On Hands From Disney's Epcot Morocco

-Herb Garden And Halloween Decorations BG Apartment Patio Surprise

-Hermit Crabs And Making Habitat For A School Project

-Hey Arnold: "I Said Hey. HEY. What A Wonderful Kind Of Day. To Love To Work And Play And Get Along With Each Other.

-Hiding Stray Cats In Our Basement

-High Tea At The Garlands

-Hobgoblin Halloween Window Sign For Victoria Woods, Fox River Grove Neighborhood Pre-Trick-Or-Treating

-Hocking Hills Ohio Kids And Moms Camping Trip

-Holding Hands And Skipping On Walks With Mom

-Holes Movie

-Holiday Celebrations

-Holocaust Museum And Education Center At Skokie

-Hologram Museum In Downtown Chicago

-Holy Name Cathedral Catholic Mass In Chicago

-Homer's Odyssey Graphic Arts BHS Door Design

-Honey Hill/Phil's Beach And The Big Slide In Wauconda

-Hook And Ring Game By The Pool At Executive Manor

-Hope Chest Filled With Heirlooms And All Your Mementos Dropped Off At Dad's For Him To Give To You

-Horse And Buggy Ride Chicago

-Horse Drawn Carriages In Chicago

-Horseback Riding In Illinois, Mexico And River Ranch, Florida

-Hostel Chicago Girl Scouts, Saw High Rise Slit Windows For Jail

-Hot Air Balloons Over Our House In The Early Mornings

-Hot Chocolate With Whipped Cream And Sprinkles Bailey's Face Mugs With Wink

-Hot Tamales Candies

-Hot Tub Soaks

-Hot Tub Hugs With Mom

-How The Grinch Stole Christmas Book And Movie

-Hubba Bubba Bubblegum

-Hugs

-Hula Hoop Contests

-Hurley Wisconsin Round Barn Heifer Cows Dogs Wolf

-Hurricane Harbor Water Amusement Park Rockford With Roller Coaster Wave Pool

-I Fly Indoor Skydiving

-I Hop for High School Graduation Dinner

-I Love You To The Beach And Back

-I Love You To The Moon And Back

-I.M.A.X. Theatre, Watching Movies On A Huge Screen

-I Spy Books

-Ice Capades Show

-Ice Cream Making

-Ice Cream, Superman Colorful At 31 Flavors/ Baskin Robbins

-Ice Cream Truck In Our Cul-De-Sac

-Ice Sculptures

-Ice Skating

-Ice Skating Lessons, Shows And Costumes

-If You Give A Cat A Cupcake Book

-If You Give A Dog A Donut Book

-If You Give A Mouse A Muffin Book

-If You Give A Pig A Pancake Book

-Igloos Made In Front Yard With Snow Brick Maker

-Illinois, Midwest State Where We Were Born And Raised

-Inchworms On The Trees

-Indian In The Cupboard Books And Series

-Indian Sari Dress Met Ladies In Our Neighborhood And Dressed Up

-Indiana Jones Movies And Halloween Costume

-Inhaler

-Insync Boy Band

-Iron Beads Art Project

-Ironing Scarves

-Italian Charms, Personalized

-Italy Family Trip

-J.F.K. Health World

-Jack Johnson Songs

-Jacks And Bouncy Balls

-Jalapeño Poppers Appetizers

-Jameson's Charhouse In Buffalo Grove

-Jan Brett Children's Books, Beautiful Illustrations

-Jane Adams 1889 Hull House Museum On Halsted Street Settlement House

-Jello Making, Many Colors And Flavors

-Jellyfish On The Beach Clear Blobs

-Jenga Stacking Block Game

-Jet Skiing At Camp Eberhart in Three Rivers, Michigan

-Jet Surfing USA In Clermont, Florida-Christmas 2023 Road Trip With Mom

-Jewelry Making

-Jewelry Mom Gave Me For UNE College Graduation

-Jewelry Boxes, Special Box Mom Made Me

-Jiffy Cake Mixes

-Jiffy Pop Popcorn

-Job Searching Indeed Help

-Johnny The Gecko

-Jokes Wood Eye Hair Lip

-Jolly Rancher Candies

-Jonas Brothers Concert-Wisconsin Summerfest Mom Surprised Me With Tickets

-Joyce's Driving School Private Lessons To Get My Driver's License

-Juice Boxes With Straws

-Jukebox, Putting In Coins And Picking Songs

-Julie Ann Frozen Custard From Crystal Lake, Illinois

-Julie's Nails Mani Pedi

-Jump Rope

-Jumping Fountains

-Jumping On Beds

-Jungle Book Movie, The Bare Necessities

-Jungle Gyms, Slides, Teeter Totters And Merry Go Rounds

-K-Mart Blue Light Special Sales

-Kaleidoscope Art School In Barrington, Illinois

-Kapok Champion Tree In Florida With Mom

-Karaoke Microphone Singing In Our Music Room

-Karate Flips At Harper

-Kelsey Road House Restaurant, Decorations, Pizza

-Kennedy Space Center-Cape Canaveral-NASA In Florida-Christmas 2023 Road Trip

-Keychains On Backpacks

-Key Lime Cove Waterpark Staycation With Mom, Lazy River

-Kickball Games

-Kings Around The Corner Card Game

-Kishwaukee Junior College, Malta, Illinois Mom Made Surprise Visits To Keep Me On The Right Track

-Kiss Girl, Mom's Pet Name For Her Beautiful Daughter

-Kit Kat Chocolate Candy Bars, Give Me A Break, Give Me A Break, Break Me Off A Piece Of That Kit Kat Bar

-Kite Flying Beese Park

-Kitten Rescues

-Kittens, Adopting And Hiding Them In The Basement

-Kitty Cats

-Knolls Apartments Nashville, Tennessee

-Kobe of Japan (Fire Choo Choo-Marble Drinks-Birthday Photos)

-Kohl's Children's Museum In Chicago

-Kohl's Department Store, Using Coupons

-Kringle Danish Pastry-Pecan From Racine, Wisconsin

-Krispy Kreme Donuts

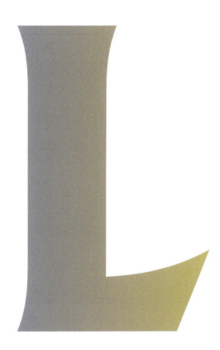

-Lady And The Tramp Stuffed Animals And Movie

-Lake Forest Bakery For French Crullers And Jelly Donuts

-Lake Forest Beach Walking Down The Steps

-Lake Forest College Circle, Where Mom Lived As A Child

-Lake Geneva, Wisconsin Boat Ride Beach Restaurant

-Lake Michigan

-Lamb's Farm In Libertyville, Illinois

-Land Before Time Dinosaur Movie Series

-Land's End Monogrammed Backpacks And Needlepoint Personalized Christmas Stockings

-Langendorf Park In Barrington, Illinois

-Lanyard Making

-Las Vegas

-Lauderdale-By-The-Sea, Florida

-Lauderdale Pier

-Laughing Until We Peed In Our Pants

-Laughter

-Laundry, Mom Always Did And Loved Doing All Our Laundry

-Laundromat Day In Fox River Grove, We Went With Mom And Took Up The Entire Laundromat

-Lavender, Mom's Favorite Smell

-Laser Tag Birthday Parties

-Lazy River Tubing

-Learning To Read

-Learning To Shave

-Lector, Mom Reading The Bible At St. Anne Church, Barrington, Illinois

-Left Bank, Pasquesi's Cheese Dogs, Mom's Childhood Hot Dog Stand In Lake Forest, Illinois

-Lefty

-Legoland Downtown Chicago And In Florida

-Legos Building Toys

-Lemonade Stand Mom Made. Even With A Built-In Cash Register

-Lemonheads Candies

-Lenny's (Denny's) 24-Hour Restaurant

-Leprechaun Book I Created

-Let's Play Dog and Owner With Mom

-Letters To Mom

-Letters To Tanya Tooth Fairy, Santa, Easter Bunny

-Library Books. So Much Fun Choosing Our Weekly Books

-Library Cards

-Library Lifetime Membership In Fox River Grove

-Licking The Mixer Attachments From Making Cake Mix

-Licking The Spoon From Making Cookie Dough

-Light Up Pumpkins With Our Names Carved In Them

-Light Up Sneakers

-Lightening And Thunder, Hiding Under The Covers With Mom And The Cats Maxie, Then Lollipop, Magic And Ellie

-Lightening Bugs

-Lighthouses. Climbing Stairs To The Top

-Lion King Movie With Simba And Scar

-Lincoln Logs And Building Houses

-Lincoln Park Zoo And The Chicago Cow Statues

-Lite Brite Electronic Art Board

-Little Boy's Bible, Read With Mom At Bedtime

-Little Girl's Bible, Read With Mom At Bedtime

-Little Mermaid Movie

-Little Tyke's Basketball Hoop In Our Front, First Floor Playroom

-Little Tyke's Cars

-Little Tyke's Playhouse

-Little Tyke's Toy Kitchen

-Little Tyke's Wagon

-Livingston Taylor, James Taylor's Brother, Mom Sung On Stage With Him 11 Times, Loving Arms Duet

-Lobster Rolls Sandwiches In Boston, MA

-Lollipops Big Round And Giant

-Lolly (Lollipop) The Yellow And White Cat, My Hansome-Man-Ny

-London Red Phone Booth Shelf Furniture For My Room

-London Vacation To Visit Grandparents

-Long Boarding Down The Road

-Long Grove Apple Fest

-Long Grove Chocolate Fest

-Loose Teeth, We Would Wiggle Them And Pull Them Out And Put Them Under Our Pillow For The Tooth Fairy

-Lottery Scratch Off-Getting All 9's And Won $100

-Lou Malnati's Pizza

-Louis Armstrong's Song Wonderful World

-Love You Forever Book

-Love You To The Moon And Back

-Lucky Charms Cereal Magically Delicious Colored Marshmallows

-Luigis Italian Ice, Lemonade Flavor

-Lunchables

-Lunches-Mom Always Wrote Note On Napkin Everyday

-Lyric Opera Seeing Performances With Mom

-M & M's Melt In Your Mouth, Not In Your Hands

-Macaroni And Cheese, Making It Myself

-Macaroni Grill Pasta Restaurant In Schaumburg

-Macrame Art Projects

-Mad Libs Joke Pad Where We Add Random Words To Make A Funny Story

-Magazine Subscriptions Nat Geo Kids

-Magic Markers

-Magic School Bus Animated TV Series Scholastic Ms. Frizzle And Her Class On Field Trips

-Magic The Calico Cat

-Magic Waters Water Park In Rockford, Illinois

-Magician, Candy Table And Special Champion Ring Notes From Everyone For 20th Birthday Party

-Magnets On The Fridge, ABC Letters To Write Words

-Magnificent Mile (Mom Would Take Us To Donate To Homeless)

-Maine Month-Long Trip To Old Orchard Beach

-Making Dinners With Mom, Measuring Out Ingredients, Mixing, Cooking And Baking, And Setting The Table, And Cleaning Up

-Making Homemade Mozzarella Balls Learned From The Chef At Barrington's Frantonio's By The Library

-Makray Memorial Golf Club (Manager Offered To Pay For Prom Dinner)

-Mama's Peas Book That Mom Wrote For Us

-Mancala Game Made With Egg Cartons And Dried Beans

-Mandelas, Calming Coloring, Gifts For Mom Which She Would Frame To Celebrate My Work And Artistic Gifts

-Manger Christmas Set Up We Would Do Every Season

-Mani Pedis At Julie's Nails

-Manicures At Julie's Nails In Fox River Grove, Illinois

-Maps On Our Basement Walls So We Could See The World

-Marbles

-Mario Tricoci Salon And Spa Day

-Markers Smelly-Big Kits

-Market Square And Fountain In Lake Forest, Illinois

-Marriott Lincolnshire Theatre Shows Plays And Musicals

-Marvelous Maine Embroidery Mom Made, Old Orchard Beach

-Mary Did You Know That Your Baby Boy Would Someday Walk On Water Song

-Mary Poppins-Movie And Musical in Chicago, Mom Got Umbrella With Bird, Practically Perfect In Every Way, Spoonful Of Sugar, Song "Don't Go To Sleep Or Close Your Eyes"

-Mascot For Saint Anne's And BHS

-Massage Chair In Our Music Room

-Matching Clothes One-Time With Mom And Brother-Sister Outfits

-Math Curse Book

-Maxie the Cat Who Died-Found In Closet-Father Jack Blessed

-McCormick Place Corvette Show In Chicago, Personalized Corvette Sweatshirt

-McDonalds Bouncy Ball House

-McDonalds French Fries With Ketchup

-McDonalds Happy Meals And Toys

-McDonalds Shamrock Shakes

-McFlurries Shakes Mixed With Candies At McDonalds

-Medical Books Where Mom Kept Track Of Our Health, Even Wrote In When We Stubbed Our Toe

-Medieval Times Horse Show And Dinner, Wearing Crowns

-Memorial Day Victoria Woods Annual Neighborhood Parade Decorating Bikes

-Men In Black Movies

-Merit Club Mother's Day Brunch-Sat In Red Corvette

-Mermaid

-Merry Christmas Blocks

-Merry Go Rounds

-Metal Detectors Mom Even Bought Me A Professional One

-Metra Train Rides From Fox River Grove To Ogilvie Train Station And Transportation Center In Chicago, Sometimes We Would Take The Train For An Adventure Just To Explore A Town Next Door

-Michael Jordan Full-Size Poster In Our Play Room

-Mickey Mouse Blanket

-Midnight Our Black Cat-Died In Operation At The Vet

-Midtown Club Swim, Sauna, Hot Tub, Tennis, Dinner Where I Filled Out Menu Form; Took Tennis-In-No-Time Class With Mom Where She Met Rick

-Midtown Surprise "Tree" Party Where Coaches And Teammates Came To See Me

-Mike & Ike Candies

-Milk Mustaches

-Milky Way Candy Bars

-Millennium Park Crown Fountain Two Huge LED Reflecting Pool Sculptures

-Milo & Otis Dog And Cat Movie Narrated By Dudley Moore

-Milwaukee Summerfest On The Wisconsin Waterfront With Concerts, Events And Food Trucks

-Miniature Golf

-Miniature Teapot Sets To Play Tea

-Minnesota Soccer Tournament-Mom Made Gifts And Snack Bags For All My Teammates

-Miracle the Baby Kitten That Survived Because Mom Performed CPR And Mouth To Mouth

-Mom's Books She Wrote, God Came To My Garage Sale And The TRUE DECEIT FALSE LOVE 8-Book Series Including This TRUE LOVE book And Her Latest Book PARENTAL ALIENATION

-Mom's Lullabies She Would Sing Us At Naptime And Bedtime And When We Were Cuddled Up In Blankets Swinging On The Outdoor Porch Swing In The Breeze

-Mom's Many Rescue Trips Out West To Help Me (Colorado, Washington State, Oklahoma)

-Mona Lisa Painting-Thought She Was God-Louvre Museum In Paris Skating With Heelies

-Monet's Garden Pop-Up Book

-Monkey Grow Kits

-Monkeys

-Monopoly Family Board Game Nights

-Monster Scary Mask At Halloween

-Montefescione, Tuscany, Italy Baseball Trip, Mom Did The Team's Laundry

-Montessori-Peel Potatoes-Making Bread

-Mood Ring

-Moon Shoes with Bungee Springs To Jump Around

-Morraine Hills State Park Cross Country Ski Trip

-Morton Arboretum Nature Hikes And Classes

-Mother-Daughter Bracelets And Necklaces

-Mother's Day, Making Cards And Homemade Gifts

-Mound Builders Creation Art Project

-Movers, OM From Fort Lauderdale To Nashville, Mom Paid To Move All My Furniture That She Bought Me

-Movie Nights

-Moving Totes And Bins, Mom Ordered For Packing

-Mozzarella Sticks In Our Lunches

-Mr. Beefy's in Fox River Grove For Hot Dogs, Gyros, Fries And Shakes, They Had A Pac-Man Game To Play

-Mr. Bubbles Bath Soap

-Mr. Potato Head Toy

-Multiplication Charts And Using Fingers For The Nines

-Museum of Contemporary Art Chicago

-Museum of Science And Industry In Chicago

-Museums

-Mushroom Soup

-Music

-Music Box Classical CDs-Hall Of The Troll King

-Music Boxes That Wind Up

-Music Room

-Musical Chairs

-My Symphony-Mom's Favorite Poem By William Henry Channing

-Mylar Balloons

-Mystic Waters Des Plaines Family Aquatic Center

-N.A.S.A. Tour In Florida See Rockets As A Kid And On Our 2023 Florida Christmas Road Trip

-Name Art Each Letter Animal Or Plant

-Names

-Naper Settlement In Naperville, Illinois

-Naps

-NASCAR 3-Lap Daytona Florida International Speedway Experience, With T-Shirts And Hat Souvenirs

-Nashville January 2024 Move To The Knolls, October 2023 Weeklong Trip For Job And Apartment Searching

-Nature Walks With Mom

-Navy Pier Ferris Wheel Photo Stained Glass Kiosks

-Needlepoint Christmas Stockings With Our Names On Them

-Neighborhood

-Neighborhood Parties, Mom Always Entertained And Was So Kind To All Our Neighbors And Friends

-Nerd Homemade Halloween Costume With Suspenders, Taking A Photo Of Myself In The Mirror

-Nerds Candies

-Nerf Guns Soft Ammunition So Nobody Would Get Hurt

-New Honda Cars From Dad For Graduations, With A Big Red Bow On Top

-New Year's Eve Stay Up, Watch TV, Sparkling Cider, Appetizers, Hats, Blow Horns, Confetti

-Newspaper Hats to Wear And Float In The Lake

-Niagra Falls (Silly Video Green Screen-Tantrum-Boat)

-Ninja Turtles Action Figures And Movie

-Noddy Character from England

-Norge Ski Jump Fox River Grove Olympic Hopefuls

-North Carolina Visit Granni's Memorial Grave

-Northern Illinois University-Mom Got Doctorate Degree In 1997

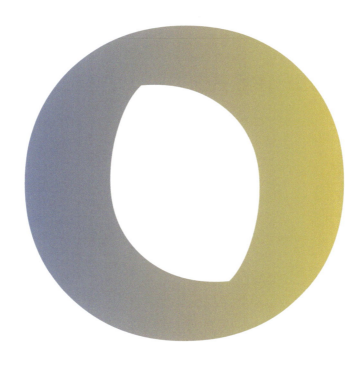

-O.T. and P. T. Occupational And Physical Therapy, Swinging On Swing To Improve Low Muscle Tone

-Oak Street Beach Chicago Crowds

-Ober Mountain Gatlinburg, Tennessee Snowboarding Planned Trip

-Oberweiss Ice Cream

-Oberweiss Milk Delivered To Our Front Porch

-Office Show We Always Laughed

-O'Hare Airport Watch Planes And Use Heelies In The Terminal

-Oklahoma Rescue, Mom Flew Out To Help Mel And She Drove Me Back To Palatine, Illinois

-Old Orchard Beach Maine Kids Club Ice Cream Shop Beach

-Old Water Tower Chicago

-Olive Garden Italian Restaurant Chain With Salads, Pasta And Warm Breadsticks

-Olives On Our Fingertips

-Omelets

-101 Dalmations Movie, My Tail Is Cold

-Onion Pub In Lake Barrington, Illinois, Loved Their Soup

-Onesies

-Oompy-Doomy of Loompy Willy Wonka Oompa-Loompas; Name Mom Would Call Me

-Orange Chocolate Ball Only At Walgreens, Holidays

-Orange Little Tikes Wagon

-Organizing Art Supplies

-Organizing Our Messy Drawers

-Oriental Trading Company Bulk Trinkets

-Origami

-Outdoor Wood Burning Brick Fireplace

-Outdoors

-Outside

-Ovengrinders Mom's Favorite Restaurant In Old Town Chicago On Clark Near Fullerton With Mediterranean Bread, Pizza Pies, Farmer's Salad

-Oz Theatre Chicago

-P.B.I. Baseball Job Professional Baseball Instruction Clean Toilets And Maintain Fields

-P.B.J. Sandwiches, Mom Would Cut The Crusts Off

-Paddle Boarding On Long Lake In Illinois

-Paintball

-Painted Clay Art Afternoons

-Painted Violin, My Artwork, That Mom Hung In Our Music Room

-Painting

-Pajama Parties And Sleepovers With Friends

-Pajamas With Feet

-Pan For Gold At Donley's Wild Wild West And In Colorado

-Pancakes Mickey Mouse Shaped And Heart Shaped

-Pancakes Silver Dollar With Hot Syrup And Butter

-Panda Express Chinese Fast Food And Orange Chicken

-Panera Bread-Greek Salad-Bread, Not Apple, Soup

-Paper Airplane Making

-Paper Chains For Our Christmas Tree

-Paper Fans Folding

-Paper Mache Christmas Ornaments Piñata Balloons Made With Flour And Water And Newspaper Strips

-Parachute Army Men To Play With, Throw From The Top Of The Stair Landing And Watch The Chute Open Up

-Paraffin Wax On Our Hands

-Parasailing In Mexico, Brother And Sister

-Parks And Recreation Funny TV Sitcom With Silly Humor

-Party City For Party Favors And Balloons

-Pasquesi's Cheese Dogs, Mom's Childhood Hot Dog Stand In Lake Forest, Illinois, Also Called The Left Bank

-Passport Photo Hunt At Many Florida CVS's

-Passports Got As Toddlers To Fly To England To Visit Grandparents And Renewed For Our Family Mexico Trips

-Pasta Eating At Macaroni Grill And Olive Garden

-Pasta Making, Mom Would Make Homemade Cheese Raviolis

-Pea Pod Grocery Deliveries

-Peace Museum In Chicago

-Peanut Butter And Jelly Sandwiches, With The Crusts Cut Off

-Peanut Butter And Marshmallow Sandwiches

-Peanut Butter Cookies Fork Crisscross Design

-Peanuts On Floor At Bills Pizza

-Pecan Pie From Baker's Square

-Pedicures At Julie's Nails In Fox River Grove, Illinois

-Peggy Notebaert Nature Museum Butterflies, Met Jane Goodall Who Was Famous For Researching Primates

-Pen Big Fat With Many Colors Click

-Pennies in Fountains-Making Wishes

-Penny Souvenir Museum Smooshed Stamped

-Penny Wishes

-Pet Rock

-Petco Lake Zurich, Illinois

-Peter Rabbit Books, Movie And Stuffed Animal

-Peter Rabbit Crib Furniture Quilt Nursery

-Petersburg Plan To Visit Elizabeth's Hometown In Central Illinois

-Petting Zoo Animals

-Phantom Of The Opera Musical At The Oakbrook Drury Lane And Marriott Lincolnshire Theatres

-Phil's Beach Honey Hill Wauconda Big Slide Sand

-Phone Booths Red London, And Shelf Curio For My Bedroom

-Phone Number 1999

-Phone Pranks

-Photo Albums

-Photo Collages

-Photos

-Piano, Black Grand In Music Room

-Piano Lessons

-Piano Recital With Mom At Barrington Library

-Picasso Sculpture Richard J. Daley Pablo Picasso

-Pick Up Sticks Table Game In Tube With Colorful Sticks

-Picking Daisies From Our Garden

-Picking Flowers For Mom

-Picking Snozzberries From Our Front Yard

-Pickles

-Picnics in the Park

-Pierced Earrings

-Pierced Ears

-Pig Kitchen Message Board

-Pigeon Carrier Who Listens In Spanish

-Pigtails With Colorful Ribbons

-Pikachu Yellow Pokemon Character

-Pillow Case Decorating/Bags For Trick-Or-Treating

-Pillow Fights

-Pillow Prayers

-Pillsbury Orange Rolsies Mom Would Always Make Us

-Pin-The-Tail-On-The-Donkey Door Game

-Pineapple Turkeys Mom Would Make, Heads Out Of Felt With Craft Eyeballs

-Ping Pong At The Milwaukee Airport

-Pinky Promises

-Pinochio

-Pinstripes Bowling At The Arboretum In South Barrington, Great Brunch

-Pipe Cleaners

-Pirates Cove Elk Grove Village

-Pistachio Nuts And Red Fingers

-Pizza From Rosatis

-Pizza Hut Personal Pan Pizzas

-Pizza Parties

-Plaid Couch

-Planetarium Telescopes Chicago Astronaut Buzz Aldrin Signed Book, Met Him

-Planting Seeds In The Garden

-Play Dates With Classmates And Neighborhood Kids

-Play Doh Clay To Play With And Put Through Tools To Make Things

-Play Kitchen, Pots And Pans, Plastic Food, Fridge

-Play Room

-Playing Doggie And Owner With Mom In The Basement

-Playing In Boxes

-Pledge Of Allegiance Sept. 11, 2011 Barrington Memorial Park Eagle Scout And Gold Award Honorees

-Plunge Beach Resort For Mother's Day On El Mar Drive In Lauderdale-By-The-Sea, When I Decided To Move To Fort Lauderdale

-Pochohontas Movie

-Poems For Mom, Mom Saved All My Poems And Artwork

-Poetry Writing Acrostics -Pokeman Trading Cards

-Pond Water Collect Analyze Tadpoles

-Pontoon Boat Rides On Long Lake

-Pony Rides

-Ponytails

-Poo Chi Electronic Dog Everyone Else Getting Polly Pocket Or Cabbage Patch Dolls

-Pooh And Tigger Photo At Disney On College Visit

-Pool Underwater Easter Egg Hunt Arlington Heights, Illinois

-Pool Rescue (Mom Jumped In With Clothes) Langendorf Park In Barrington, Illinois To Save Me When I Couldn't Swim

-Poop Stuck, Painful, So Thankful That Mom Manually Helped Because Laxatives, Prunes And Stool Softener Didn't Work

-Pop Rocks Candies

-Popcorn At The Movies

-Popcorn Balls At Halloween

-Popcorn Chicken KFC

-Popcorn, Homemade And Put In Lunch Sacks, Snuck Into Movie Theaters To Save Money

-Poppies 1st Flower In Our Garden, Mom's Favorite Red Flower

-Pops That Came In All Sorts Of Colors

-Popsicles, Red White And Blue Rockets And Banana And Fun

-Poptarts

-Porch Swing

-Port Edward Restaurant Algonquin Boat In Middle Koi And Goldfish

-Portillos Restaurant For Italian Beef Hot Dogs Salad With Pasta

-Possum Skidaddaling At Palatine Townhouse

-Post Cards From Mom

-Post Office To Mail Grandparent Cards

-Posters For Bedroom

-Potato Peeling At Barrington Montessori School

-Potato Sack Races

-Potato Salad, Mom Made The Best Homemade

-Potholders We Would Make With Weaving Tool And Rings Of Fabric

-Pots And Pans Band With Wooden Spoon Drumsticks

-Potty Training Targets In Toilet Soft Seat, Stool, Charts And Rewards

-Power Ranger Red Gift For Brother At Sister's Birth

-Power Rangers Pajamas

-Power Rangers Red And Blue Halloween Action Figures

-Pram England Buggy/Stroller Mom Restored

-Prayer Pillows

-Prayer Time At Bedtime

-Praying

-Pringles With Ranch Dip

-Prom (Hers) With Limo

-Prom (His) With Group

-Pudding Making, Vanilla And Chocolate

-Puddle Splashing In Our Rubber Boots

-Puddles

-Puffer Fish

-Pulling Loose Teeth

-Pumpkin Carving

-Pumpkin Picking

-Pumpkin Pie With Whipped Cream

-Pumpkin Seed Roasting

-Pumpkins

-Purple Bag In Closet Small Toys For Friends When It Was Time For Them To Go Home

-Putting Lost Teeth Under The Pillow At Night

-Puzzles

-Quarter Collection From All 50 States

-Quarters-Mom Got Me $300 Worth For Doing Laundry Each Time She Visited Me In Fort Lauderdale

-Quicksand, Sinking And Getting Stuck

-Quiet Moments

-Quig's Apple Orchard With Cinnamon Donuts In Mundelein, Illinois

-Quiltmaking Books And Blankets From Mom

-Quilt-Mom Made With Pillowcases From Our St. Anne's Sweatshirts

-Quilts Mom Made Us For Our Baby Nursery

-Racecars, I Would Keep Many In My Pants Pockets

-Racetracks

-Racine, Wisconsin Pecan Danish Pastry Kringles

-Radios

-Rain Boots Splashing In Puddles

-Rainbow Fish Art Birthday Party And Cake

-Rainbow Fish Book And TV Show And Sweatshirt Mom Made

-Rainbows and Playing in the Rain

-Raindrops Keep Falling On My Head Song

-Raking Leaves Into Piles And Smelling Leaves Burning

-Rapture Birds of Prey

-Ravinia Concerts Picnic Near Highland Park, Illinois

-Razor A-Kick Scooter

-Record/LP Collection From Mom And Her Mom, My Granni, Many Were Classics And Valuable, Left In Oklahoma With The Special Record Player Mom Got Me

-Record Players

-Red Balloon Book And Movie With No Words

-Red London Phone Booth Shelves For Bedroom

-Red Rover Neighborhood Game

-Reeses Peanut Butter Cups Candy

-Reindeer Ears On Van

-Reindeer Ears With Lights Mom Got Me For My Christmas Tree Job In Fort Lauderdale

-Remote Control Cars, Helicopters

-Remotes TV, When Lost We Had To Get Up To Change The Channel

-Renaissance Medieval Fair In Wisconsin, Eating Turkey Drumsticks, Everyone Spoke With Accents And Dressed Up

-Rent Help From Mom

-Rescues Colorado, Washington, Oklahoma

-Rescuing Our Cats Lucky And Magic From Our Backyard

-Resumes Mom Would Always Make And Update For Our Job Searches

-Reubens, Mom Made The Best Swiss, Corned Beef And Sauerkraut Sandwiches

-Ricky's Pet Shop Barrington Crickets For Gecko, Fish And Hampsters

-Riflery At Camp Eberhardt In Three Rivers, Michigan

-Ring Made For Mom In Barrington High School Metal Art Class

-Ringing Bell When Sick So Mom Would Come Check On Me

-River Ranch Rodeo In Florida, Christmas 2023 Road Trip With Mom, Met Cute Girls, Saw Wild Horses, Got My First Cowboy Hat And Bolo, Saw A Herd Of Buffalo

-Rivers

-Riverwoods Forest Preserve

-Road Trip With Mom Where I Got To Pick Where To Go With No Set Travel Plan

-Robert Frost Poetry From Mom's Childhood Book

-Rock Candy On Strings Or Sticks

-Rock Climbing YMCA, Cabela's REI, Bass Pro Shops Outdoor Store, Even On A Cruise

-Rock Painting

-Rocking Chair Naps With Mom

-Rockford Clock Tower Restaurant For Lunch

-Rollerblading

-Rollerskating

-Rolling Stone Magazine Vintage 1968 John Lennon And Yoko Ono Naked 25 Cents

-Rolsies-Orange Pillsbury Breakfast Rolls With Orange Frosting

-Room Re-Arranging School Art Project Measure Furniture

-Rootbeer Floats

-Rosatis Pizza Delivered To Our Home

-Royal Caribbean Cruise With Mom, So Much Fun

-Royal Gorge Family Trip

-Royal Rally At Palatine High School

-Run For The Border (Taco Bell)

-S'Mores Over The Campfire, Graham Crackers, Hershey's Chocolate And Marshmallows

-Safety Town Summer Camp

-Saganaki Flaming Greek Cheese, Mom Would Make At Home And I Learned How To Make It In The Microwave

-Salamanders In The Backside Window Wells

-Salt Dough Ornaments

-Sand Art In Small Bottles With Colored Sand

-Sandcastles

-Santa Hats

-Santa, The Real One

-Santa's Christmas Chalk Stand Countdown

-Santa's Lists-Asking For A Nicer Sibling And Always Asking For Mom's Wish Of Peace On Earth

-Santa's Treats Hot Chocolate, Cookies, Notes And Carrots For Rudolph The Reindeer By The Fireplace

-Santa's Village

-Sapphires Mom And Dad's September Birthstones

-Sari From India

-Savers Thrift Stores

-Scarecrow Making For The Backyard Garden

-Scared Of The Dark So Sleep in Parent's Bed, Then Later In A Sleeping Bag At Foot Of Bed

-Scarves Ironing And Folding

-Scary Movies

-Scary Stories (To Tell In The Dark)

-Scavenger Hunts In The Neighborhood And In Town

-Schaumburg Marriott Staycation With Mom

-Schaumburg Water Works Indoor Pools And Slides

-Schedules

-School Bus Waving Out Of The Window Mom Wanted To Follow

-School Lockers

-School Photos

-Schoolhouse School Photo Frames

-Science Fair Projects

-Scrabble Board Game And Mom's Art Projects

-Scrapbooks

-Scrubs Animal Hospital Uniforms For Every Season

-Sea Glass Collection

-Sea World In Florida Orca Killer Whale Splash

-Seafood Tower At Nashville's Ruth Chris Steakhouse

-Seal's Batman Song Kiss From A Rose

-Sears Tower Chicago Sky Deck 103rd Floor Observation Box

-Second City Laughing Comedy Club Kid's Show

-See 4 States From Chicago Sears Tower, Now Called The Willis Tower

-Sewing Buttons On Clothes

-Shakespeare Bathroom With Books, Art And Teapot

-Shamrock Green Shakes At McDonald's

-Shaving For The First Time

-Shedd Aquarium In Chicago

-Shel Silverstein Books The Giving Tree, Where The Sidewalk Ends, A Light In The Attic. Black And White Simple Drawings And Poems

-Shell Frame Made In Easton, Maryland

-Shooting Stars

-Shoveling Snow

-Shrimp All-You-Can-Peel And Eat

-Sidewalk Chalk Drawing

-Sign Language Learn Alphabet Using Our Hands And Fingers

-Silence And Quiet Time

-Silhouettes from Wilmette For Music Room

-Silly Bands Shapes Animals Bracelets Trend

-Silly Putty

-Silly String Spray Can Bright Colors Mess

-Singing In The Car

-Singing In The Shower

-"Sink Sink" Mom Would Say For Something Hot

-Sippy Cups Cups With Built-In Straws

-Skateboarding

-Ski Jacket The Viking Ski Shop In Barrington, Illinois, Mom Bought It Special For Me Even Though It Was Expensive

-Skip-It Game

-Skipping Stones

-Skittles Candies

-Slacklining And Balancing Between Trees

-Sledding In Fox River Grove Ski Hill

-Sleepovers With Friends

-Sleigh Rides At Farms

-Slides, Climbing Up The Ladder Stairs And Gliding Down

-Slime Make Ourselves With White Glue, Baking Soda And Saline

-Slime Mini-Men Throw On Wall

-Slimy Salamanders In Our Back Window Wells

-Slinky Metal Rings On The Stairs

-Slip-and-Slide Water Mat In The Front Yard

-Slurpies Slushy Drinks From 7-11

-Slushy Machine

-Smells Sensitive

-Smelly Markers

-Smiley Face Cookies, Huge, Yellow And Delicious

-Smoothies Healthy

-S'mores with Graham Crackers, Hershey's Chocolate Bars And Marshmallows

-Smurfs-Blue Elf Guys

-Snake In The House, Under Covers Watching TV

-Snakes

-Snapping Turtle in Middle Of Kelsey Road, Mom Moved Him Off The Road With A Cushion

-Snickers Candy Bars Satisfies You

-Snorkeling In Cancun, Mexico

-Snow Angels Made From Lying Down In The Snowy Yard

-Snow Cones with Rainbow Fruit Juice Colors

-Snow Days Off Of School, So Excited When The Call Came In

-Snow Globes Make Our Own

-Snow Suits Land's End Red With Blue Neck Gators

-Snow White And The Seven Dwarves Movie

-Snowboarding At Devil's Head In Wisconsin And Winter Park In Denver, Colorado

-Snowman The Movie And Book, Just Music, No Words, Song Flying In The Sky High-Pitched Voice

-Snozz-Berries From Willie Wonka And Our Garden

-Snuggles

-Snuggling With Mom

-Soarin' Over California Ride At Disney

-Soccer Coach Mom Was My Recreational Soccer Coach One Season

-Soccer Balls

-Soccer Games

-Soccer Goalie (Beese Park) Red Sports Goggles For Glasses

-Soccer Team BASA And Barrington High School

-Soccer Tournaments, Mom Would Chaperone And Make Art Project Gifts For All My Teammates

-Sock Hop Dance And Costumes

-Sorry Board Game

-Sound Of Music Movie, The Hills Are Alive, Doe A Deer…

-Sounds, Sensitive To Loud Sounds

-Sour Patch Candy

-Spa, Our Backyard Outdoor Hot Tub, I Would Cuddle Up With Mom In The Hot Water While We Listened To Soft Music In The Darkness

-Spa Day

-Space Jam Song And Movie With Michael Jordan And Bugs Bunny, Dancing On The Tables

-Sparkling Apple Cider

-Sparky Barrington's 4th Of July Dalmatian Fire Truck

-Speech Therapy

-Spice House Evanston Favorite Place For Cooking Seasonings

-Spices On Pantry Wall

-Spiderman Action Figure, Comic Book And Movie, And Costume

-Spin Art With Colorful Paint

-Spirograph Drawing Tools, Circles With Designs

-Splashing in Puddles On Rainy Days

-SpongeBob Squarepants TV Show

-Sportsmart For Sports Equipment

-Springfield, Missouri Trip To Blue Eye/Cambridge To Meet Great Aunt And Great Grandma

-Sprinklers, Running Through Them

-Sprouts Grocery Store Delivery Nashville From Mom

-Sprouts Growing In Large Mason Jar, Healthy

-Spy Gear

-Spy Kids Movies

-Squirt Guns

-St. Anne Chapel And Church Barrington, Illinois

-St. Anne School, Barrington, Illinois

-St. Anne Sweatshirt Quilts Made By Mom

-St. Louis Arch Missouri Road Trip And Soccer Tournament

-St. Patrick's Day Fun

-Stained Glass In Our Kitchen Window Garden

-Stamp Collecting, Started But Lost Interest

-Stamping Art With Cut Potato at Cornerstone's Montessori School

-Stand Up Paddle Boarding at Long Lake, Illinois

-Standing on Stools To Wash Dishes

-Star Wars Movie Series And DVDs

-Star Wars Toy Light Savers

-Starbucks "Double Chocolate Frappuccino"

-Starbucks Drive Through Before School

-Starburst Candies

-Stars "Star Light Star Bright, First Star I See Tonight" And Watching Shooting Stars

-Starved Rock State Park Oglesby, IL, Beautiful Waterfall And Hike

-State Quarters Collection

-Stickers

-Stork Wooden Display To Announce Birth In The Front Yard

-Stranger In The Woods Deer Book Photos Stuffed Animals

-Strawberries Dipped In Chocolate, Mom's Specialty

-Strawberry Milk

-Strawberry Picking Thompson's Farm Wisconsin

-Straws

-String Game Using Both Hands And A Thin Rope

-Stuffed Animals

-Subway Italian Footlong Sandwiches

-Summer School Each Grade Activities Summer Learning Head Start

-Sunsets Watching From Our Porch While We Would Swing On Our Double Porch Swing

-Super Heroes

-Super Mom-Daughter Scrapbook Made For Mom In 2020

-Super Soaker Water Gun

-Superman Comic Books

-Susan Branch Book Baby Love Met Author At Barrington Book Signing, Heart Of The Home And Vineyard Seasons

-Swan Boats In Boston, Massachusetts, Also Cheers Bar, Harvard, Quincy Market And Faneuil Hall, Street Performers In The Square

-Swearing

-Swedish Fish Candies

-Sweet Tarts Candies

-Sweetie Ding, Mom's Pet Name For Her Handsome Son

-Swimming Classes At The YMCA

-Swimming Pools

-Swinging On The Front Porch

-Sword In The Stone Movie

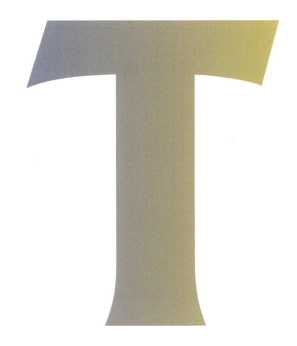

-TJ Maxx For Housewares And Sadler Teapot Collection

-Taco Bell (Run For The Border)

-Tamagotchi 1990's Toy Tech Digital Pet, Attach Keychain Over 80 Million Sold

-Tang Orange Powder Drink

-Tater Tots

-Tattoo Moon Done By Scooby From Prescott, Washington, Mother-Son Handshake, Held Up My Hand On A FaceTime When I Needed Help

-Tattoos

-Tea Party Book Collection

-Teapot Collection, Sadler Company From England

-Teapot Window Showcase At Barrington Library

-Teeter Totters

-Temporary Tattoos

-Ten Second Tidy Comfy Couch Dust Bunnies, Messy Room, Challenge To Encourage Us To Clean Our Rooms

-Ten Speed Bike

-Tennis In No Time, Took Tennis Lessons With Mom At The Midtown Club in Palatine, Illinois, Where We Met Rick

-Tennis Shoes I Colored With Markers

-Terrarium Projects, Growing A Mini Eco System

-Texts Telling Mom How Much I Love Her

-Thank You Notes

-Thanksgiving, Eating Turkey, Mashed Potatoes, Green Bean Casserole, Cranberry Sauce And Pumpkin Pie

-The Giving Tree Book By Shel Silverstein

-The Notebook (Romantic And Sad Movie)

-The Very Hungry Caterpillar Book

-Theme 2 (My Regular Order Was NOT On The Menu)

-Thinker Statue Also Weight Of The World On My Shoulders

-Thomas The Tank TV Show And Toys

-Thumbelina Movie

-Thumbprint Artwork

-Thumbs Up

-Thunderstorms

-Tic Tac Toe Games On Paper Placemats At Restaurants

-Tic Tacs Orange Or Fruit Candies

-Tie Dye T-Shirts

-Tiger-Gave a Tiger A Baby Bottle To Drink

-To Infinity And Beyond From Buzz Lightyear

-To The Beach And Back

-To The Moon And Back

-Toaster Strudels From The Freezer

-Tollhouse Chocolate Chip Cookies

-Tomato Growing In Mom's Garden

-Tomato Soup And Grilled Cheese

-Tooth Fairy (Tanya-Silver Dollars Or $2 bills)

-Towel Hoodies For After Bathtime

-Toy Car Collections

-Toy Cars Stuffed In Pants Pockets

-Toy Store F. A. Schwartz, Too Expensive, Only Window-Shopped

-Toy Stores

-Toy Story, Buzz Lightyear To Infinity And Beyond, Woody

-Toy Story Movie And Disney Theme Park Area

-Toys R Us

-Tracing Letters Sand Shaving Cream

-Trader Joes Grocery Store

-Trail Mix And Making GORP (Granola, Oats, Raisins And Peanuts)

-Training Wheels On Our First Two-Wheeler Bikes

-Trampoline Park

-Trampolines Mini And Big

-Travel Baseball

-Travel Soccer

-Tree Artwork

-Tree Climbing And Gear

-Tree Forts

-Tree Identification And Books From Mom

-Tree Shelves In Fort Lauderdale

-Trevi Fountain In Italy, Making A Wish By Throwing A Coin Backwards Into The Fountain

-Tribune Tower On Michigan Avenue In Downtown Chicago

-Trick-Or-Treating in Victoria Woods

-Trolley Museum Fox River In Elgin

-Trolls Under Bridge To Our Pink Backyard Playhouse

-Truck 18-Wheeler After Focus Karate Lessons, Practicing Driving With Permit as Truck Almost Hit Our Car, Saved By An Angel

-Truck Stop Souvenirs

-Trucks

-True Love

-Trumpet Lessons At St. Anne's, In The Band

-Trust Fall

-Tuesday Morning Store Shopping In Fox River Grove, Illinois

-Tunnel Tents

-Turtle Hatching At 5 AM In Our Front Yard Landscaping, Mom Let Me Stay Home From School To Take Care Of The Baby Turtles

-Twentieth Surprise Birthday Bash With A Musician And Lots Of Friends

-Twister Floor Game

-Two Dollar Bills

-Two Wheeler Bikes

-Typewriter, Mom Teaching Us To Type

-UGG Boots, Mom Bought Me My First Pair

-Umbrellas, So Much Fun Choosing The Style

-Unconditional Love, Mom's Love Is To The Moon And Back

-UNO Card Game

-VHS Tapes Movies Disney

-Vacations

-Valentine's Day Tissue Or Shoe Boxes Decorated

-Van Chrysler Gold with Big Wreath On Front For Christmas

-Vatican In Rome On Italy Baseball Trip

-Vegetables "Eat Your Vegetables" Mom Would Say And Had A Special Wooden Sign She Made On Her Garden Gate

-Velcro Toss And Catch

-Velveteen Rabbit Book And Tape

-Very Hungry Caterpillar Book

-Vet Visits For Our Cat Check Ups

-View Master Old Fashioned Hand Slide Show

-Villa Olivia Bartlett Skiing With The Girl Scouts

-Village Squire Restaurant For Saganaki In Crystal Lake, Illinois

-Vitamins Chewable, Different Animal Shapes

-Volcano Baking Soda With Vinegar

-Volleyball St. Anne's, Mom Was One Of The Scorekeepers

-Volleyball Team

-Volo Museum Antique Cars "I Want That Car" From Chitty Chitty Bang Bang

-Vortex Football

-Waffle Cones Better Than Safety Cones Or Sugar Cones

-Waffles, Frozen Leggo My Eggo

-Waiting For The School Bus

-Walker Brothers Original Pancake House

-Walkie Talkies Homemade Cup And String

-Walmart For Power Shopping

-Washer And Dryer At Knolls In Nashville Paid By Mom

-Washing Dishes

-Washington DC Arlington Cemetery Cherry Blossoms

-Washington State, Bellevue, Rescue, Mom Saved My Life

-Water Gun Fights

-Water Is Wide Song/Lullaby Mom Would Sing Us To Sleep

-Water Parks

-Water Skiing At Camp Eberhart In Three Rivers, Michigan

-Water Slides

-Water Tower Place Deli Long Menu Take Escalators To Top Floor

-Waterfalls And Camping In Hocking Hills, Ohio

-Watermelon Use Outer Skin As Bowl

-Wax Mini Juices Candy

-Wax Molds Souvenir Museum Dinosaur Feel Hot

-We Are The World Song With Michael Jackson And Many Singers

-What A Wonderful World Song By Louis Armstrong

-Wheelbarrow Races On The Front Lawn

-Where The Wild Things Are Book

-Where's Waldo Books

-Whistling

-White Chocolate Cross Candy For Easter

-White House Tour In Washington, DC

-White Sox Games At The Old Cominsky Park

-Whitewater Rafting Family Trip In Colorado

-Whittling Walking Sticks In Hocking Hills, Ohio

-Who Let The Dogs Out Song "Who Who Who Who"

-Whoopie Cushion Making Farting Sounds

-Wicked-The Broadway Musical In Chicago

-Wild Horses At The River Ranch Rodeo In Florida

-Wild Onion Pub In Lake Barrington

-Wild Wild West Town Donley's In Union, Illinois Panning For Gold, Watching Cowboy Shoot Out, Horseback Roping Lesson And Tomahawk Throw

-Willow Creek Church Graduations

-Willy Wonka Movie (Oompa Loompa- Veruka Salt Wanted A Goose That Laid Golden Eggs For Easter)

-Wilmot, Wisconsin Ski Trips After School

-Window Boxes Filled With Flowers Cascading From Our Bedrooms

-Window Ledge And Getting Stitches By Eyebrow From Jumping Too Far

-Window Shades Made By Mom So Our Rooms Were Dark for Naps

-Window Stickers

-Winking

-Wisconsin Cheese

-Wisconsin Dells Trips

-Wisconsin Racine Kringles, Pecan Was Mom's Favorite

-Wisconsin Road Trips

-Wisconsin Strawberry Picking At Thompson's Farm

-Wishbones From Turkeys At Thanksgiving And Trying To Get Largest Side

-Wishing Tree At The Fox River Grove Library, Mom Would Have Us Donate A Gift Every Time We Went To Check Out A Book

-Wizard of Oz Play And Movie

-Wood Burning Fireplace At Victoria Woods And The Knolls

-Woodfield Mall Skipping The Shopping, Just Seeing Stores In Strollers

-Woodstock Town Square Farmer's Market Lunch At The Old Prison

-Wooly Willy Magnetic Face Game

-Word Search Puzzles Wreath Making

-Wreath On Front Of Car At Christmas

-Wreaths On Front Door For Every Holiday

-Wrigley Field In Chicago

-Wristbands

-Writing Stories About Being A Vet

-Wynken Blinken And Nod Story

-X-Rays At Good Shepherd Hospital

-Yellow School Bus To Go To School

-Yellow Submarine Song From The Beatles

-YMCA Days-Off-School Program

-YMCA Swimming Lessons With Mom

-Yo-Yo Tricks

-Yoga At Fort Lauderdale Beach And The Plunge Resort

-"You Rock" Handmade Frame And Scrapbook For Mom

-Yurt Geodesic Dome Tent For Girl Scout Camping

-Zion Beach Illinois State Park

-Ziplining With Mom

-Zoo Animals

-Zucchini Growing In Mom's Garden

*"Never blame anyone in your life. Good people give you happiness. Bad people give you experience. Worst people give you a lesson. And best people give you memories."*

**~ *Zig Ziglar*,**

*American Author, Salesman & Motivational Speaker*

"This is what I like best about photographs: they're proof that once, even for just a heartbeat, everything was perfect."

~ **Jodi Picoult,**

*American Writer of Novels, Short Stories & Issues of Wonder Woman*

---

"Photography is the art of making memories tangible."

~ **Destin Sparks,** *Photographer*

---

"The best thing about a picture is that it never changes, even when the people in it do."

~ **Andy Warhol,**

*American Artist & Film Director*

---

"Photography is a way of feeling, of touching, of loving. What you have caught on film is captured forever. It remembers little things, long after you have forgotten everything."

~ **Aaron Siskind,** *American Photographer*

# PHOTOGRAPHS & MEMORIES

*"Lookin' back on how it was in years gone by and the good times that we had. Makes today seem rather sad, so much has changed. Those were such happy times and not so long ago. How I wondered where they'd gone. All my best memories, come back clearly to me. Some can even make me cry. Just like before, it's yesterday once more."*

**~ *The Carpenters*,**

*American Brother-Sister & Vocal-Instrumental Duo*

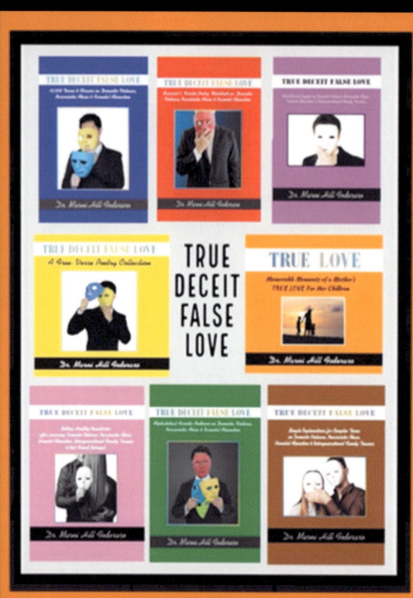
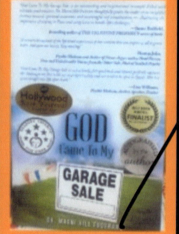

# M♥M's BOOKS

# M💜M loves you both!

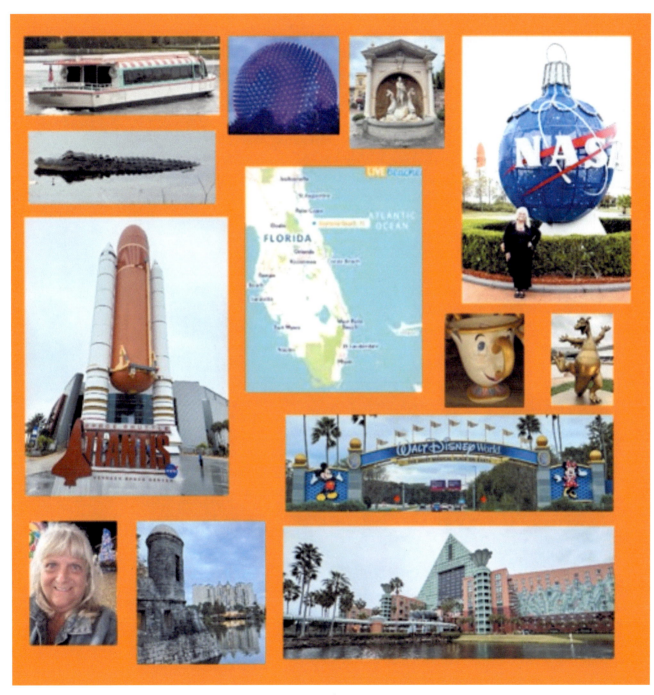

# MY HOME IN FRG, IL
## 1148 VICTORIA DR.

Squeeze the lemon

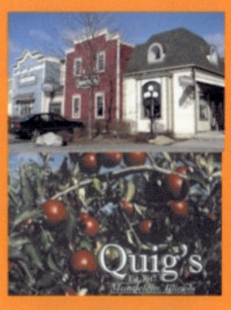

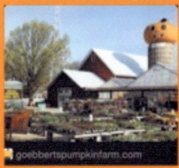

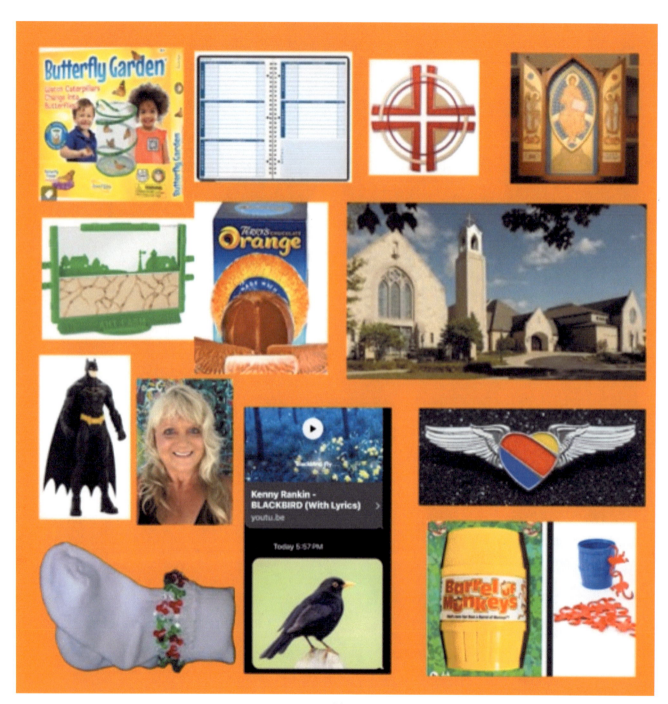

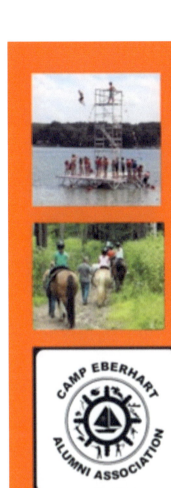

FUN

**Mother's Love**

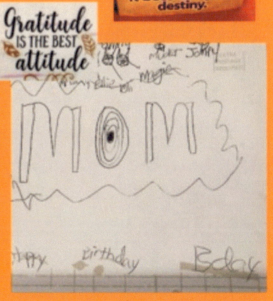

Ariana Grand Concert surprise

😃 Fake bird's egg!

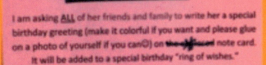

💚
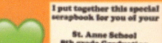

# MY HOME IN FRG, IL
## 1148 VICTORIA DR.

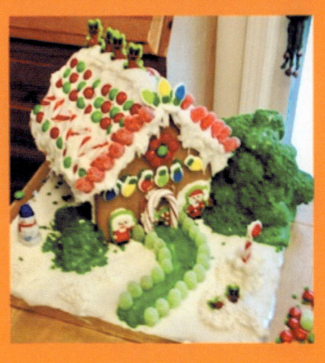

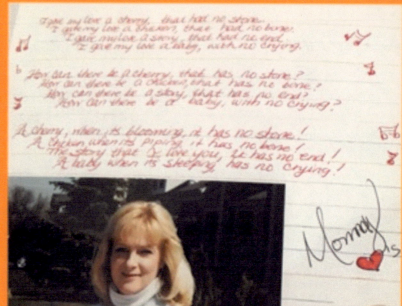

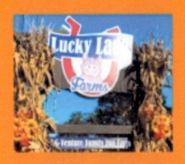

**TN**

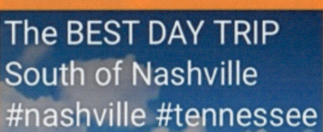

The BEST DAY TRIP South of Nashville #nashville #tennessee

## My son

I wish you the strength to face challenges with confidence...along with the wisdom to choose your battles carefully...I wish you adventure on your journey and may you always stop to help someone along the way...listen to your heart and take risks carefully...

Remember how much you are loved...I am so proud of you!

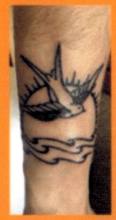

Call your mother. Tell her you love her. Remember, you're the only person who knows what her heart sounds like from the inside.

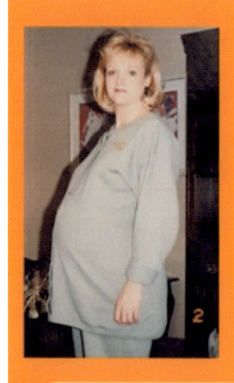

cut off a lock of hair

1st haircut

BABY CL...

Wow! What a closet

**BABY'S FIRST CLOTHES**
soft, snuggly, and sweet

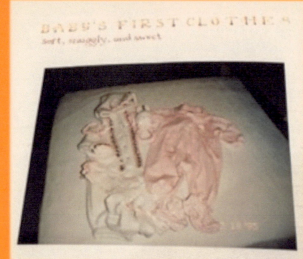

the love between a mother and daughter is forever

# Mother's Day 2023

Glad you're going to use your critical thinking skills to realize the truth that it makes common sense that loving parents want and encourage their kids to have a positive sibling relationship with each other.

You are a very resourceful, hardworking, caring and handsome man, and gosh-darn it, people like you!

I LOVE YOU!
💕 U2 🌙&🌏

Always,

M💜M

Happy Saturday night. 🎷 Hope you are doing well. 💕

Soooo looking forward to seeing you for Mother's Day tomorrow. 🍾🎁

Take good care of yourself. You are a wonderful person and I am proud of you.

I LOVE YOU to the moon and back!

Always, M💜M

I will come by your apartment at 10 am. We will have a great brunch 🥞🍳🥓 at Blue Moon. 🌙

See you in the morning ☀️ Sweety Ding!😊

Love,

M💜M

& M💜M

Thank you for your beautiful Mother's Day card! 📖🌺

I loved seeing you, going to our favorite Blue Moon brunch 🥞🦀 and spending time together at Flamingo Gardens. 🦩

making Christmas cookies

← christmas comfort food

← mom's 2001 Honda CRV

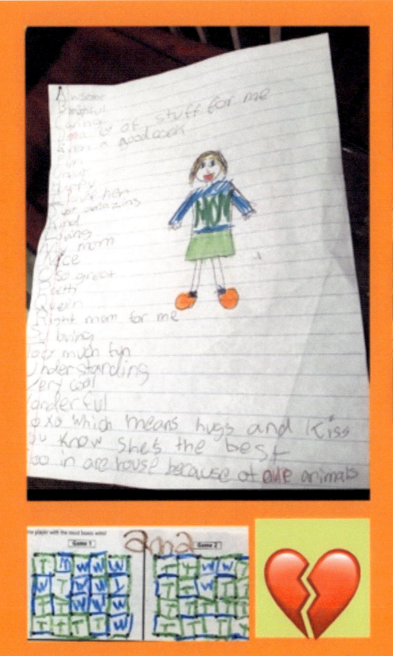

Last photo with both of our children

this is mommy's favorite song to sing to you!

the rest goes:

♪♫ Now there's a ship... and she sails the sea...
she's loaded deep... as deep can be...
but not so deep... as the love I'm in...
I know not how... to sink or swim...

Love is handsome... and love is kind
the sweetest flower... when first it's new...
but love grows old... and waxes cold...
and fades away... like summer dew.

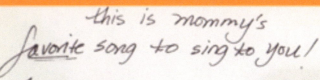

Thinking of you!

i love you unconditionally

Dear St. Nicholas,

I don't want anthing in my shoe. I only want peace on earth.

Friends forever,

Merry chitimass

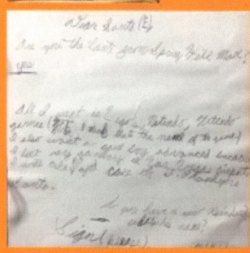

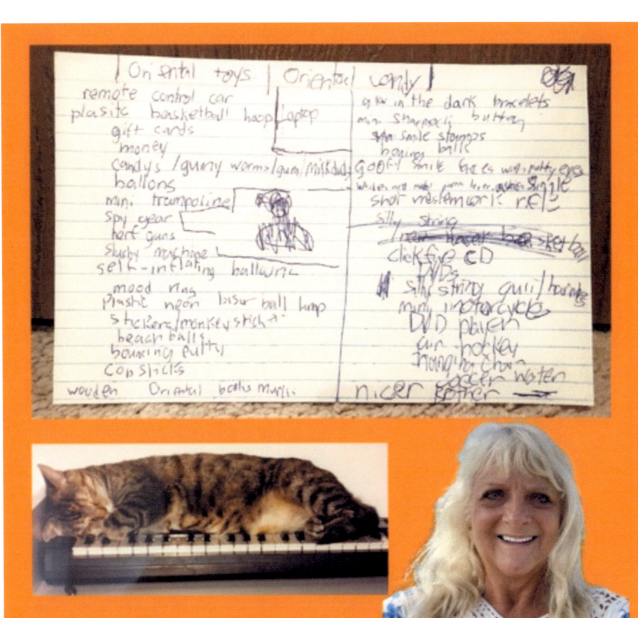

meows & music

*champion ring*

### Dear, Mom
Thank you for always being there for me. Like the time I was sick and you help me. Also the time you help me with my homework. And all my toys you gave me like my bike.

Thank you for my cats you let me have. Because I always love them and play with them. Also for letting me go to birthday parties.and that's what I'm thankful for.

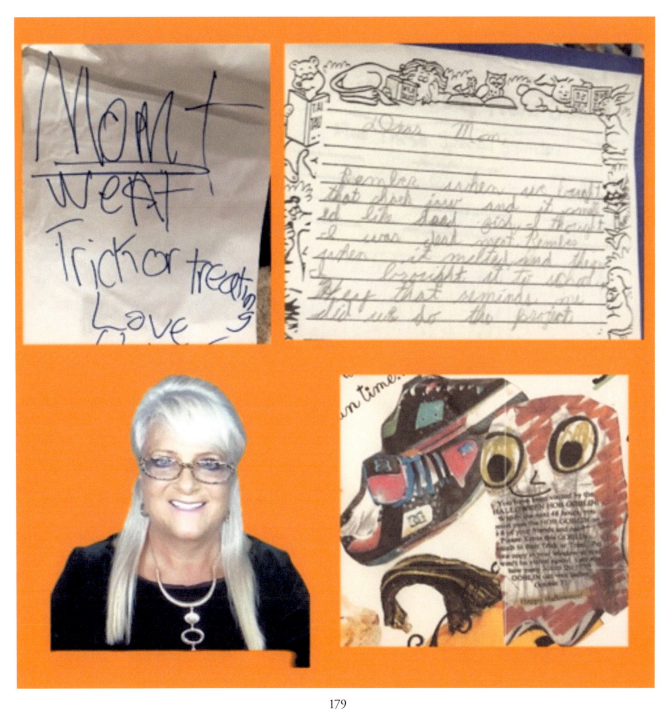

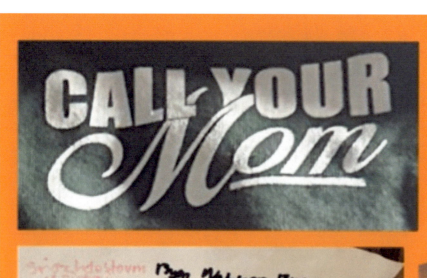

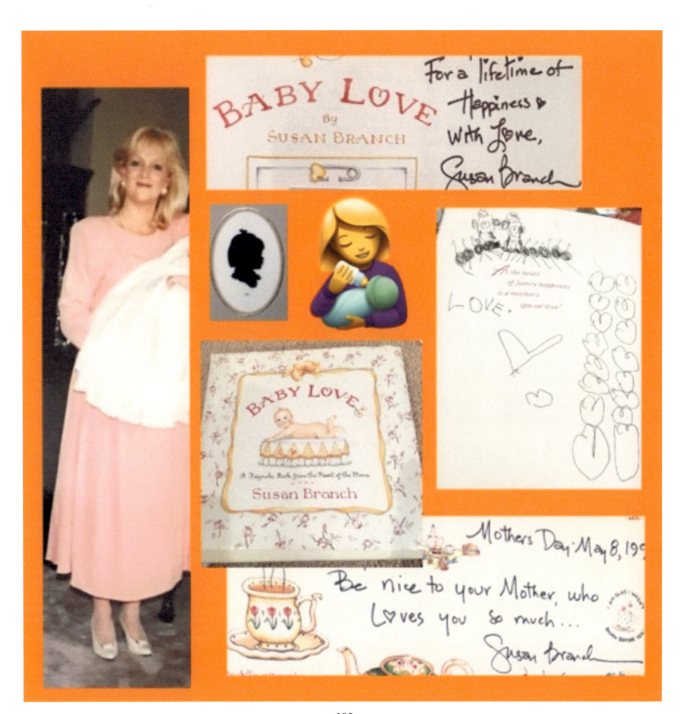

*Christmas mornings*

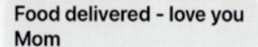

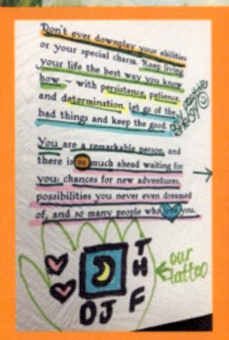

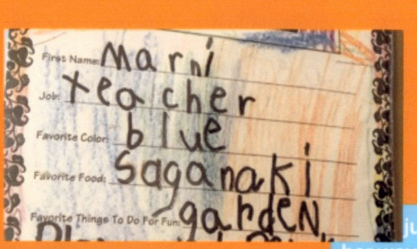

ALWAYS HAVE HOPE 🍀 PRAY 🙏 AND BE THE BEST PERSON YOU CAN BE 🌈 WITH LOVE 💕 IN YOUR HEART.

Be happy 😃 and believe in Honesty and Goodness!

Love you to the moon and back. I look at my/our tattoo everyday. 💕 U2🌙&🌍...M❤️M

...just needs to find her way and is trying to survive Alienation 💔💰; it's not her fault...we should forgive her and we shouldn't blame her. Deep down she knows the truth and of our love ❤️ for her.

She's studying psychology 📚 and in time will learn about Parent Alienation and Narcissist Abuse.

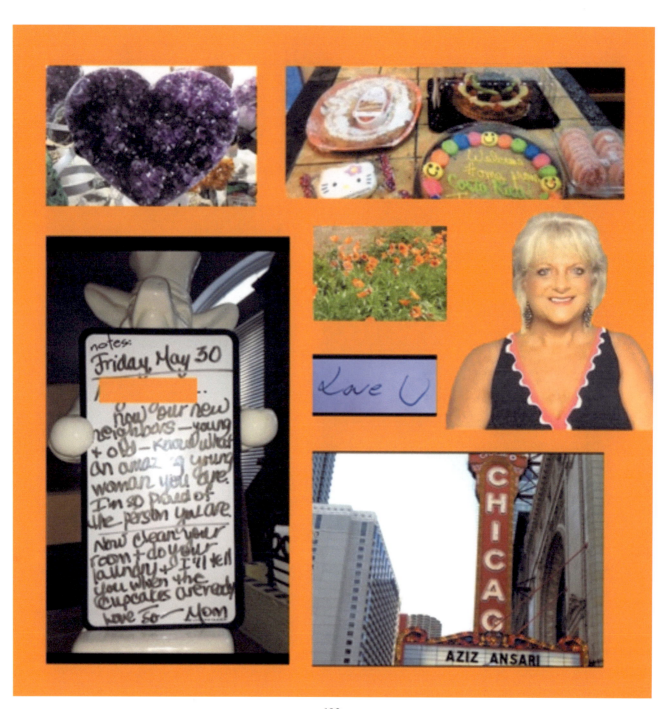

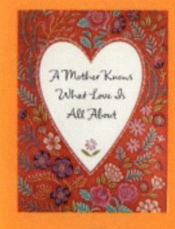

My heart breaks because we used to be so very close. I hope we reunite in this lifetime. If not, someday she will realize that she broke my heart and missed her adult years having a relationship with her mom.

> Happy 4th 🇺🇸🎖️🇺🇸🎖️🍔
> 🎆🌭 love you...M💜M

Read 9:29 AM

Happy 4th Mom

Love you 🍿🎊🎊

> 💕U2🌙&⭐M💜M

> this is a great video to watch to help build your independence, understanding and happiness. 🇺🇸 K, you are WORTHY and GREAT just being yourself. I am so proud of you. Believe in yourself. You are a wonderful human being and I love you just the way you are. Always, M💜M

**LOVE**

"Mom, when you move my hair like that I can't see my dream"

make a wish

**Secret O' Life - James Taylor**
youtu.be

M❤️M's favorite song🎼

**James Taylor - Line 'em Up (Live)**
youtu.be

One of our car songs: Line them up by James Taylor

FUN

*"Mary, did you know...that your baby boy....."*

God will bring her back to us. 🙏 She will come to know that it's okay to love BOTH parents and her brother (amazing YOU 👦 💕 😊 ), Grandad

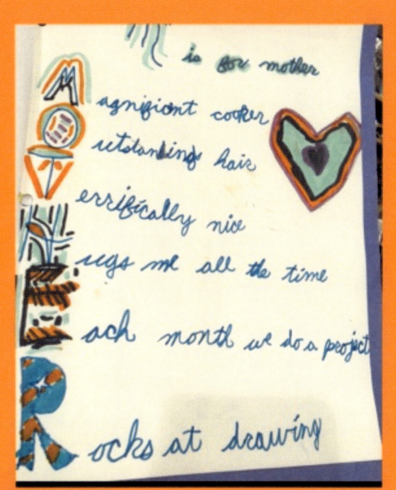

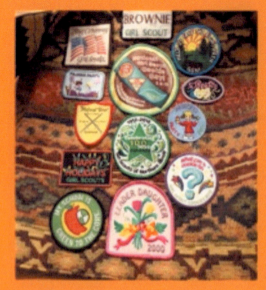

213

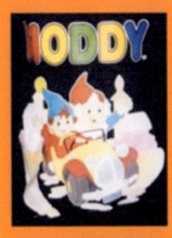

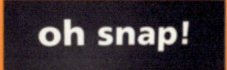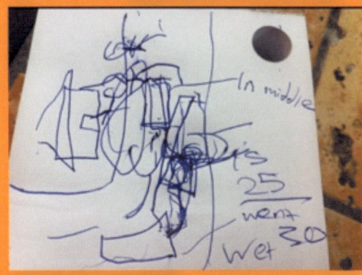

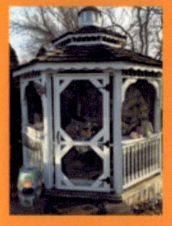

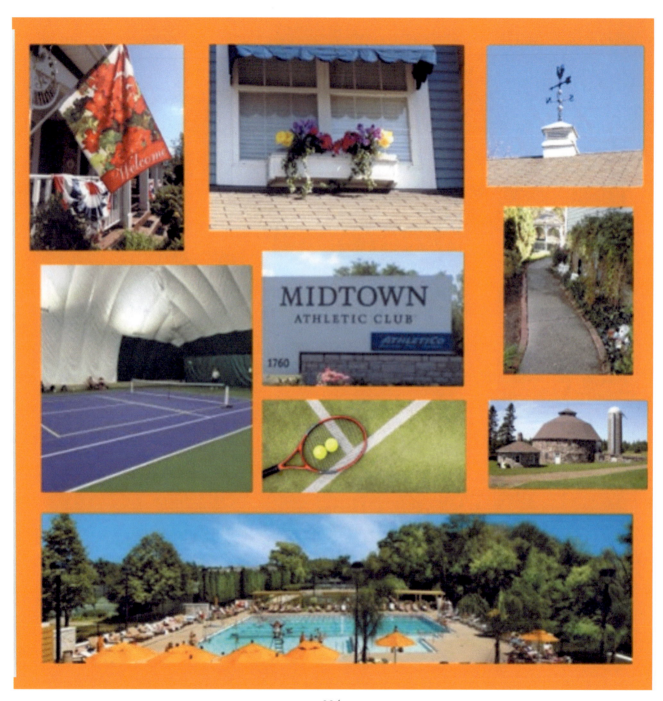

"Champion ring"

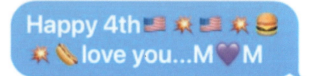

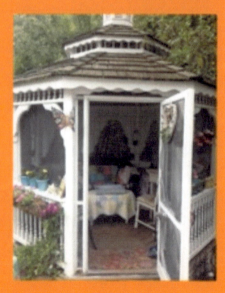

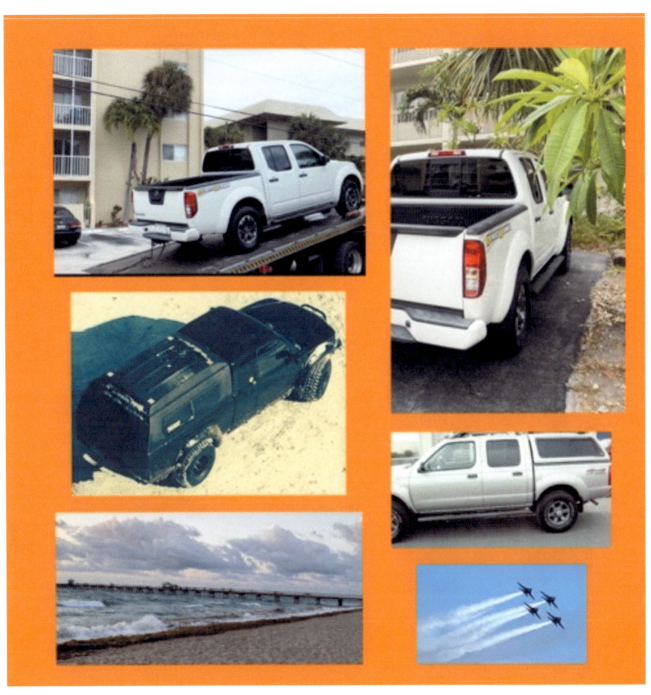

I have not heard your voice in years, but my heart has conversations with you every day.

# Marvelous Maine

## Hand-Stitched by Mom

Joy be with you while you stay
And peace be with you on your way

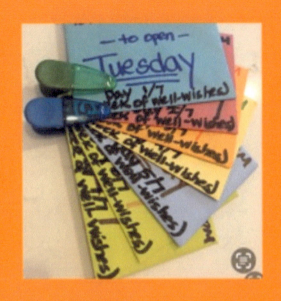

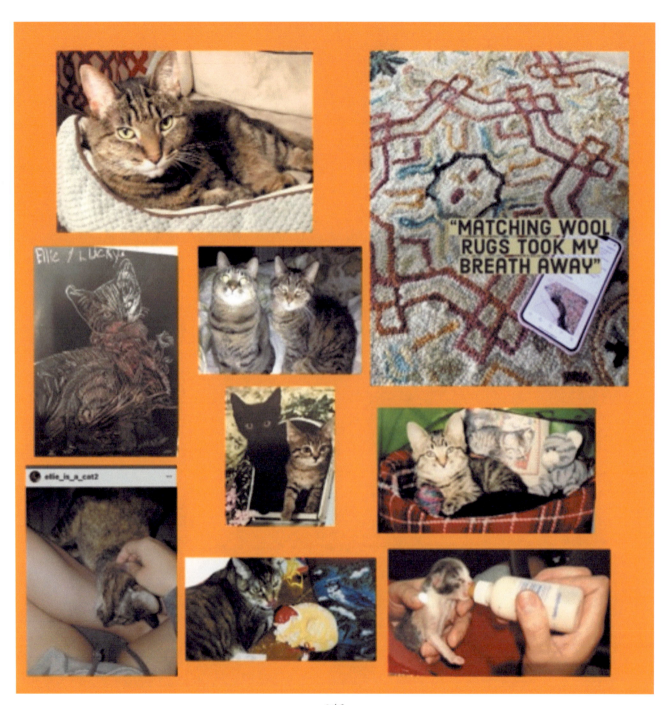

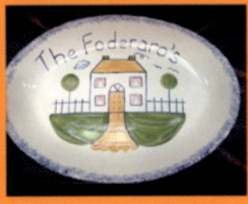

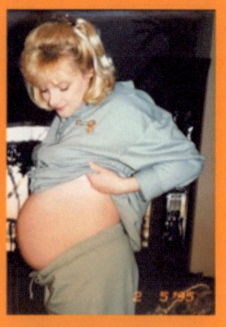
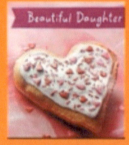
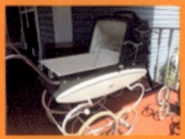

# Mom 💜s you!

# M💜M loves you both!

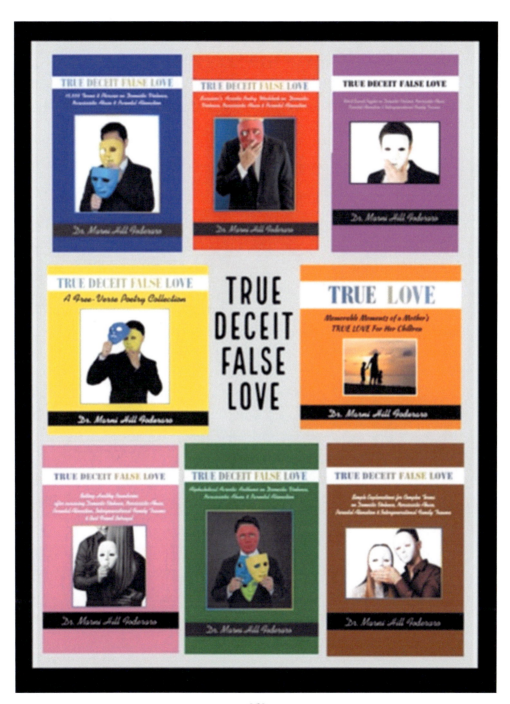

# www.GodCameToMyGarageSale.com

## https://www.amazon.com/author/drmarnihillfoderaro

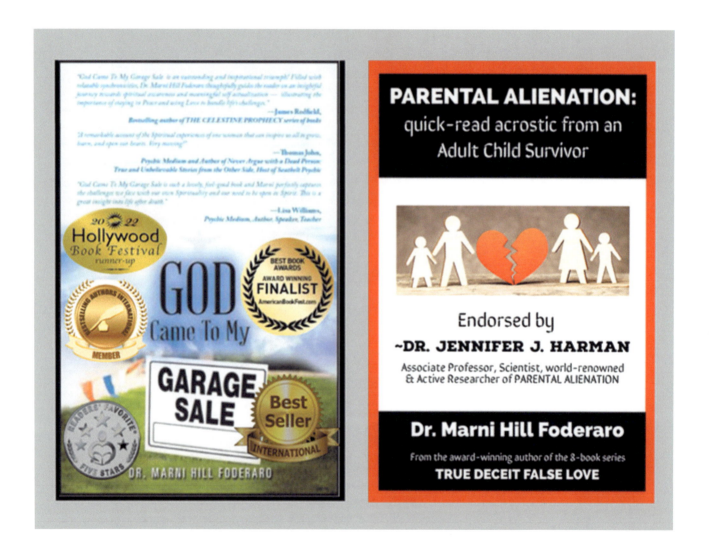

*"And I'll take with me the memories to be my sunshine after the rain. It's so hard to say goodbye to yesterday."*

**~ Boys II Men,**

*American Vocal Harmony Group*

Printed in the United States
by Baker & Taylor Publisher Services